Managing Electronic Resources:
New and Changing Roles for Libraries

CHANDOS
INFORMATION PROFESSIONAL SERIES

Series Editor: Ruth Rikowski
(email: Rikowskigr@aol.com)

Chandos' new series of books are aimed at the busy information professional. They have been specially commissioned to provide the reader with an authoritative view of current thinking. They are designed to provide easy-to-read and (most importantly) practical coverage of topics that are of interest to librarians and other information professionals. If you would like a full listing of current and forthcoming titles, please visit our web site **www.chandospublishing.com** or contact Hannah Grace-Williams on email info@chandospublishing.com or telephone number +44 (0) 1993 848726.

New authors: we are always pleased to receive ideas for new titles; if you would like to write a book for Chandos, please contact Dr Glyn Jones on email gjones@chandospublishing.com or telephone number +44 (0) 1993 848726.

Bulk orders: some organisations buy a number of copies of our books. If you are interested in doing this, we would be pleased to discuss a discount. Please contact Hannah Grace-Williams on email info@chandospublishing.com or telephone number +44 (0) 1993 848726.

Managing Electronic Resources:
New and Changing Roles for Libraries

PETER M. WEBSTER

Chandos Publishing
Oxford · England

Chandos Publishing (Oxford) Limited
TBAC Business Centre
Avenue 4
Station Lane
Witney
Oxford OX28 4BN
UK
Tel: +44 (0) 1993 848726 Fax: +44 (0) 1865 884448
Email: info@chandospublishing.com
www.chandospublishing.com

First published in Great Britain in 2008

ISBN:
978 1 84334 368 4 (paperback)
978 1 84334 369 1 (hardback)
1 84334 368 1 (paperback)
1 84334 369 X (hardback)

© Peter M. Webster, 2008

British Library Cataloguing-in-Publication Data.
A catalogue record for this book is available from the British Library.

Typeset by Avocet Typeset, Chilton, Aylesbury, Bucks.
Printed in the UK and USA.

Dedication

This book is dedicated with love and gratitude to Miriam and Gillian.

Contents

Contents

List of figures

Acknowledgements

The author gratefully acknowledges the support and good advice of everyone at the Patrick Power Library and Saint Mary's University, as well as the hard working partners in the Novanet library consortium in Nova Scotia and the Atlantic Scholarly Information Network (ASIN) in Atlantic Canada.

About the author

Peter Webster has been Systems Librarian for the Patrick Power Library at Saint Mary's University in Halifax, Nova Scotia, Canada, since 1993. He holds a Masters degree in Library Science as well as a Certificate in Computer Science from Dalhousie University, Canada, and a Bachelors degree in History and English from the University of Alberta, Canada.

He has been a member of the Board of Directors, management and technical committees for the Novanet consortium of academic libraries in Nova Scotia. He also works closely with the Atlantic Scholarly Information Network (ASIN) regional consortium in Atlantic Canada. He has presented on library automation issues at conferences, including the Library and Information Technology (LITA) National Forum, ACCESS, The American Library Association (ALA), The Canadian Library Association (CLA) and the Atlantic Provinces Library Association (APLA).

Peter Webster's recent articles include "Challenges for federated searching" (*Internet Reference Services Quarterly*, 12(3/4), 2007), "The library in your toolbar" (*Library Journal*, 15 July 2007), and "Interconnected and innovative libraries: factors tying libraries more closely together" (*Library Trends*, 54(3), 2006).

When not working to build better library services, Peter

and his wife Gillian find time for sea kayaking, hiking and biking in Nova Scotia and elsewhere also the Eastern Seaboard, as well as travelling further afield.

Introduction

Like many librarians of my generation, my career so far has been focused on building electronic collections that offer library users more material, and easier access to material, than ever before. In a little over a decade, the university library I work for has gone from offering access to a few thousand paper journals to offering tens of thousands of full-text electronic serials. While books and many other paper materials have diminished modestly in popularity, electronic collections are growing rapidly and becoming ever more diverse. Electronic journal collections continue to expand to the point where academic journals are nearly universally available online, and their primary means of delivery is electronic. Many libraries have exclusively electric current journal collections, or nearly so. Many other kinds of electronic materials are also growing in importance, including e-books, reference materials and many kinds of local deposit materials.

At the same time, electronic materials have transformed library collections, and the World Wide Web has transformed the way we all seek and retrieve information and the way we communicate and relate to information. The Internet provides a common electronic information environment and a uniform online infrastructure that is nearly universally accessible to library users. Users of the World Wide Web have embraced new possibilities and come to their information seeking with new expectations. Library services are judged against the best available services on the Internet, information resources such as Google and Amazon. What we see as daily users of online services is that all online services are compared to other available online resources. Innovations in one popular web resource raise expectations for all other online services. Advances in electronic journal interfaces drive innovations in federated search software and raise expectations for innovations in integrated library systems, and visa versa. In this innovative environment, libraries are offering a host of new "Web 2.0" methods for searching and delivering services and materials, and allowing users to interact with that information in new ways.

In the last decade, my library, like so many others, has seen the quantity and nature of the materials that we manage and mediate expand greatly and become far more complex. The library's collections have been transformed as we have moved from locally-accessed physical materials, owned in perpetuity, to online collections of leased and licensed, as well as owned "virtual" materials accessed from many local and remote sources. The library community has been addressing these changes in many ways. Our material management practices have evolved a great deal in recent years.

However, our methods continue to be centred on the integrated library system (ILS) and machine-readable cataloguing (MARC). We use essentially manual methods developed for paper collections (Figure 1.1). Although we have adapted these methods a great deal, they are increasingly lagging behind the needs of our new collections

Figure 1.1   The basic library catalogue model

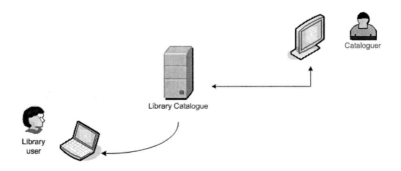

and the networked environment. Our practices are proving to be ineffective in dealing with the pace, volume and diversity of electronic materials. Many digital collections are outside the scope of traditional library collecting. They require management approaches that are not dealt with by our existing practices and that are beyond the capabilities of an ILS. As search and retrieval methods evolve, the library's materials management methods are not meeting the demands of the latest access methods. In my library, we are working hard to move beyond reacting to the demands of new library collections as they arrive. We are beginning to develop processes that can deal with the demands of online materials and accommodate future changes.

A new model for managing electronic materials has emerged (Figure 1.2). Management and delivery of our electronic library collections has become dependent not on one monolithic library system, but on many interconnected library and vendor maintained systems. Rather than focusing on one central repository, the emerging distributed and decentralised model relies on storage of management information and metadata in several different repositories

Figure 1.2 The emerging distributed library catalogue model

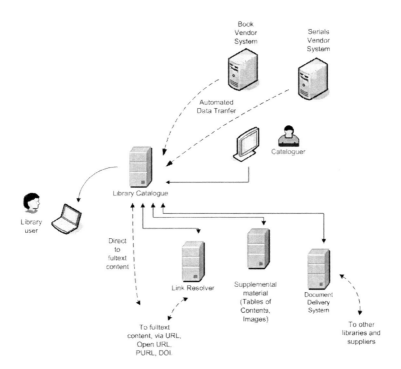

that are closely integrated to share and exchange information. This model builds on our ability to search multiple resources simultaneously and relies extensively on the linking of information between repositories to offer users an increasingly seamless search and access experience.

The new distributed approach to electronic materials management is an important part of the library's larger effort to create a more unified information environment. It underpins efforts to provide more integrated search and retrieval services. We manage electronic materials from a host of different sources every day. We work hard to reduce users' confusion over these multiple sources and to meet their expectations for convenience and simplicity. The goal of providing more seamless search and retrieval becomes something of a measuring stick with which libraries can evaluate management practices and set future directions. This book will look at how the distributed model is evolving. Although the distributed environment is firmly established, there is still much functionality that is essential for the success of the new management model that is not yet widely available. We will consider system developments as well as changes in library practice that are still needed to allow libraries to keep pace with a changing environment and changing access methods. The book will focus particularly on the sustainability of our management practices, as online collections and management demands grow, they must be balanced against limited budgets and staff resources.

The new model, in which many systems exchange information, can only be fully developed through a new level of cooperation between a large number of partners including libraries, ILS vendors, book and subscription agents, publishers, e-content aggregators, search interface and link resolver suppliers. A key component of the emerging distributed model is the automated sharing of information between these partners. This book will consider the directions that libraries and information services companies will need to take, as we continue to address the new demands.

Many libraries are fundamentally re-evaluating their activities in light of the new information environment. The National and State Libraries of Australasia have summed up their response in a document titled "The Big Bang: creating the new library universe".

New technologies are affecting every aspect of libraries. We have responded by implementing and extraordinary range of continuous improvement and innovative projects, building on the foundation of decades of collaborative technology and standards. We have created new services and made key parts of our collections available globally.

We are now in a position to explode and reshape our core services, resourcing and infrastructure; to explore radical new approaches across all parts of our work; and to fundamentally shift our libraries to the digital world. Our response to the environment is maturing and we must re-examine our collections; the services we provide to library users; our preservation and digitization responsibilities; operational priorities; and workforce planning. (National & State Libraries Australasia, 2007)

A number of important issues concerning the electronic information environment are being widely discussed in the library literature and debated in online forums.

The functionality limitations of ILSs and online public access catalogues (OPACs) have been a topic of extensive discussion. The early discussion of the distributed search environment has centred on the strengths and weaknesses of federated search software. But as libraries are developing many innovative ways to search and link multiple online resources together, it is clear that issues related to distributed search are far reaching. The shortcomings of library cataloguing practices are also being extensively debated. Karen Calhoun's report, "The Changing Nature of the Catalogue and Its Integration with Other Discovery Tools" produced for the US' Library of Congress, has been one focal point for this discussion (Calhoun, 2006). Two commentators, Andrew Pace and Roy Tennant, have been leading critics of the shortcomings of ILSs and the usability of OPACs. They have also been key innovators in library systems. Lorcan Dempsey is another key commentator who has articulated many elements of emerging information environment. It seems that many people are pursuing difference aspects of the new distributed information environment, as libraries explore the great possibilities, in addition to the great challenges, of this environment.

The rapid changes that libraries are encountering are evident even in the language used to discuss their offerings. A term like "library holdings" has a diminished meaning in an environment where much of what libraries offer is online material, licensed or otherwise accessed, rather than being physically held by the library. In the same way, the term "library collections" has had to take on a more far-reaching meaning than ever before. We often resort to common terms such as indexing and abstracting databases, or full-text databases to describe an increasingly complex selection of content sources, repositories, search tools and portals. OPAC is coming to be a much less useful term as libraries offer a number of important search interfaces that search many resources; the library local holdings database being only one. The term ILS is particularly annoying to some, as these systems are often not well integrated with a host of other important resources.

The new electronic resource management (ERM) systems have come on the scene, but vendors such as Ebsco and Serials Solutions are now describing their electronic materials management tools more broadly as "e-resource access and management services" (ERAMS) (Serials Solutions, undated). Art Rhyno and Mark Leggott have discussed replacing the library ILS with something called an "open library applications framework" (OLAF) (Rhyno, 2003). One must suspect that they selected the name chiefly because they like the acronym. Their concept of a flexible inter-connected group of systems built around common standards is a good representation of what is beginning to emerge and needs to be fostered in libraries.

We have not yet developed commonly-agreed language to describe the integrated and distributed sources and services libraries now offer or the multi-application modular management tool sets that we are developing to deal with electronic resources. New terms will no doubt emerge to describe the diverse bodies of material libraries now steward. We will continue to use commonly understood terms like collections and ILS until better alternatives come along.

2

Universal discovery and access to information

Several closely-related goals underlie the developments taking place in electronic materials and the information environment. Libraries need to examine and clearly understand these goals as they consider future directions. As libraries seek to exploit the opportunities of the new online information environment, there is a growing need for better articulated and commonly agreed strategic directions. Because without a clear set of goals, libraries will continue to react to changes in the information environment rather than setting a far reaching proactive course for their services.

The effort to develop more universal discovery and retrieval of information is the first major goal that is driving innovations in information services. Internet searching, as successfully developed by search engines such as Google and Yahoo!, has been an important step in the movement toward universal discovery. The popular idea of one-stop shopping, central or single searching as described by federated search applications are aspects of a single broad goal, the ability to easily and conveniently find all information, and the notion that a single search should locate all available material. The idea of universal searching is a natural outcome of the capabilities of the World Wide Web. Major efforts to digitise book collections, movement of more and more journals indexing to the World Wide Web – these are all part of an ongoing movement toward universal search. Despite numerous major digitisation efforts and explosive growth of web-accessible materials, the ability to search literally "everything", all recorded information, with a single web search will remain a complex and illusive goal for some time yet. There are still technological as well as political, economic and social barriers to universal access that will remain so long as content creators and owners seek to protect their valuable product and receive maximum compensation for it. However, the idea of universal search has captured the public imagination. It is obvious to users of the World Wide Web that if some materials are indexed and discoverable by web search, it is possible for all materials to be found this way.

2.1 Building a unified information environment

An element of the movement toward ultimate universal discovery and retrieval is the effort to create a more unified information environment, that is an environment where all information can be discovered and accessed using common search methods. The success of web searching came about because people were able to access diverse information using a common search method without any need to understand the format, type, structure or context of the information they seek. They seek a unified environment where there are no barriers presented by different software needs, different formats, or vendors.

The unified information environment is an easy and perhaps overly obvious concept to grasp. It is much more difficult to achieve. Information resources of all kinds are closely inter-related and interdependent. Developments in one area such as web search have an effect in other areas such as academic serials. Changes to academic search technology, such as the development of link resolving, have an effect on the services required of web search. Therefore, it is increasingly important to view the environment as a whole.

The Joint Information Systems Committee (JISC), one of the primary educational information technology development agencies in the UK, lists the information environment as one of eight strategic themes it concentrates on. JISC describes the core theme of the information environment as follows.

> There is now a critical mass of digital information resources that can be used to support researchers, learners, teachers and administrators in their work and study. The production of information is on the increase and ways to deal with this effectively are required. There is the need to ensure that quality information is not lost amongst the masses of digital data created everyday. If we can continue to improve the management, interrogation and serving of "quality" information there is huge potential to enhance knowledge creation across learning and research communities.

> The aim of the Information Environment is to help provide convenient access to resources for research and learning using resource discovery and resource management tools and the development of better

services and practice. The Information Environment aims to allow discovery, access and use of resources for research and learning irrespective of their location. (JISC, 2007a)

JISC also maintains a committee that focuses on the integrated information environment, described as follows.

JISC Integrated Information Environment committee is responsible for ensuring the continued development of an online information environment to provide secure and convenient access to a comprehensive collection of scholarly and educational material, building on existing partnerships and forging new ones to contribute to a vision of a single, worldwide information environment. (JISC, 2007b)

OCLC in the USA has also focused attention on "the Information Landscape" in a series of Environmental Scans (Wilson, 2003). Their scan breaks down the environment to consider several landscapes, including the technological, economic and social. OCLC extends the environmental metaphor by discussing the information ecology. The National and State Libraries of Australasia chose to think in terms of the "library universe" (National and State Libraries of Australasia, 2007). There is a growing consensus that libraries must be thinking in terms of the information environment as a whole, and planning our services within the context of that environment. There are many issues related to electronic information that are most effectively dealt with at the level of the global information environment.

2.2 Silo busting: integrating management and access to online information

Today's networked information environment is not unified; it is a complex collection of different media and different formats requiring many software applications. A large and intricate collection of information exchange protocols, presentation formats and programming languages have been devised to give the World Wide Web its appearance of uniformity. The information resources that libraries offer are even more diverse and fragmented than the public Internet. They include a stunning array of different sources that includes publisher websites, content aggregator databases, individual electronic publications, collections of digital objects and e-books. Each has its own independent information storage formats and indexing methods. Each has its own user interface, presenting users with hundreds of information interfaces. Libraries offer large amounts of indexing or abstracting mixed with actual "full-text" content. They feature a not very orderly mixture of paper materials and electronic materials.

Most of the tools that have advanced library service in the last few years – information exchange standards; federated searching; link resolving technology; new search interfaces and library catalogue enhancements – are methods of better integrating diverse information offerings. Many of the information sources libraries offer are carefully and deliberately separated and kept in a proprietary manner. The business models of library vendors rely on keeping systems separate. Business practice is to closely guard technical innovations from competitors. Competing companies work to differentiate their services from one another, to promote the superiority of their product, and to encourage customers to deal as much as possible with one vendor. Despite recent advances, ILSs remain discrete proprietary systems, not designed to easily share information with other systems. They were created to integrate cataloguing, circulation and acquisitions functions. They achieve this internal integration with closed, proprietary systems. The price of good interaction between the different library functions has been little external openness and interoperability.

The many independent and proprietary content products that make up library online collections have been described as information silos; that is, independent vertical columns of information closed and largely cut off from one another. The array of silos offered by libraries present a confusing and inconvenient environment for service users. They must be familiar with multiple interfaces and confront an array of accessibility barriers as they seek information across diverse systems. Making information easy to find across a multitude of individual online systems, in addition to breaking down barriers between those systems and rendering the differences between silos invisible to users, has been a central goal of business information systems for several years now. Formal and informal applications standards, from database standards to common word processing and spreadsheet document standards, are part of the long-standing efforts of the computer software industry (in particular, the open source software movement) to break down barriers between silos.

For the foreseeable future, integrating diverse information to foster a more unified information environment will be a central and over-riding role for libraries. Over the coming years, our efforts must focus on tying many parts of the e-content environment together into a consistent whole to create a seamless experience for information seekers. The goal must be to render invisible the entire carefully maintained infrastructure that stands between searchers and information as well as distinctions between material formats and different content products. Systematically identifying and breaking down information silos whenever and whenever possible should become central library activities. A commitment to silo busting means reducing the number of online interfaces we use to search and access electronic information. It also means finding ways to exchange information between silos, and link them together.

Libraries have made some progress in unifying the information environment and removing barriers between information silos. Standards such as the Z39.50 library search standard, the National Circulation Interchange Protocol (Part 1) (NCIP) the standard for exchanging patron-related information between different systems, the SRW/U XML-based federated search interchange standard, or the OpenURL linking standard have been major steps forward. However, is important to realise just how far libraries still have to go in their integration efforts. Libraries have been slow to make extensive use of integration standards and methods. They have therefore placed relatively little pressure on vendors to fully develop them. The process of improving the functioning of new standardised services often waits until substantial numbers of libraries are using them.

Until many libraries are interested in new standardised features, there is little business incentive for information services vendors to develop them. There is a business advantage for online services vendors to keep their services proprietary. It can takes years for standards such as NCIP or SRW/U to be fully and uniformly implemented. Despite recent efforts at integration, library collections of electronic materials are continuing to become more fragmented, not less. New independent and proprietary online resources are created every day. Information seekers intuitively see information as uniform. Differences in software, content vendor, format and search interface are unnecessary impediments to seamless access. So library online resources are often seen by users as overly complex.

Silo busting can be achieved in many ways. Libraries have been quite successful in merging formerly independent collections by cataloguing them together in the library catalogue. We will continue to break down silos by merging them in different ways, cataloguing them together in the library catalogue, or using common indexing methods, or searching multiple resources with a single federated search. Each approach has its strengths and its weaknesses. Adding cataloguing records to the library catalogue for online materials held in many other online repositories, such as full-text databases is a common way that libraries link silos of information together. This approach is having immediate benefits. Nevertheless, on its own, this approach is time consuming; it becomes increasingly unwieldy as the amount of material grows and it is ultimately just creating a bigger silo. Federated searching is limited in its search capabilities, so far. Metadata harvesting or simple webpage indexing by Google and other search engines also have their shortcomings. Therefore, while breaking down barriers between online systems remains an important goal and principle, there is no single best way to achieve it.

From a management perspective, our integration efforts rely on utilising metadata about all the disparate materials that each library can provide access to. This metadata is now held in many different repositories, including library systems, content providers repositories and shared repositories such as Crossref or Open WorldCat.

Making effective use of all of these sources of information requires the access and exchange of information between groups of separate management systems. As the environment of library materials has become more complex, our need to integrate administrative information that is held in many systems and locations has become as important as the integration of public resources. It is also increasingly important to avoid duplication in multiple repositories. More streamlined ways are needed for collecting metadata, moving it from one repository to another and amending it as it changes. Therefore, integration and automation of materials management systems and processes will be a key survival strategy for libraries in the coming years, just as integration of the public search and retrieval experience is critical to meeting the needs of library users.

2.3 The traditional integrating role of the library taken to new heights

Fostering more universal access to online information has become a central role for libraries. Silo busting in all its forms is an important part of this effort. This is not really a new role for libraries. It is a long-standing role given new scope and possibility by the new network technology. Providing unified discovery and access to information has always been a core mission of libraries. Jens Thorhauge recently stated, "The basic vision for access that I probably share with most of my colleagues is not new. It can be expressed most concisely as access for everybody to all published material, no matter how it is stored. At least for print, this vision has been behind the International Federation of Library Associations and

Institutions' (IFLA) core program, Universal Availability of Publications (UAP), for decades" (Thorhauge, 2003). ILSs were created to provide a unified search for the formerly disparate collections held in library buildings. Library consortia and union catalogues were created to extend unified search and retrieval to greater collections of materials. Today's work to integrate electronic resources is an extension of a long-standing library role.

A body of research, from OCLC's Environmental Scan (Wilson, 2003), to Ruth Vondracek's recent article "Comfort and convenience? Why students choose alternatives to the library" (Vondracek, 2007), confirms that in a world with ready access to Google and a host of online information sources, library catalogues and library services are often not the first place people turn for information.

Writing in OCLC Abstracts, Kurt De Belder, University Librarian at Leiden in the Netherlands, recently noted that:

> "Libraries are working hard for their users – introducing new services and technologies for users, making more content available". He said that library usage is up, operations are more efficient and effective than ever, and users seem to appreciate all that libraries are doing. "Library life is good", said Mr De Belder. "But we are starting to notice some fault lines in the last few years".

> He said libraries have got to "make metadata and data work for libraries" so that libraries can be as successful with users as information providers such as Amazon.com, Yahoo! and Google. "We've noticed in libraries that a lot of our information has been compartmentalized – it has been put into databases

that are not accessible and not findable through the Internet", noted Mr De Belder. "If it is not in Google or Yahoo!, our customers get the sense that it does not exist". (OCLC Abstracts, 2005)

Library service developers have responded to this in a number of ways. They are working to make the library OPAC and library services on the web better, more functional and more compelling to users, with products such as Endeca and Aquabrowser. Libraries are also offering search services from a wide range of online locations, and finding ways to integrate library services into information seekers online work stream. Library services must continue to improve if they are to meet users' changing needs and expectations. The demand for more convenient and functional search and access services is driving the need for more effective materials management.

The possibilities of the World Wide Web have not meant a declining role for libraries. Quite the reverse in fact. The new information environment is providing libraries with many important new or expanded roles. It offers a host of new avenues for information delivery, and new methods for offering the materials that libraries steward. Libraries have taken on an expanding search and retrieval role, and the new role of delivering greatly expanded collections. They have taken on a new role of delivering materials beyond the walls of the library, across college and university campus, and to library users' home desktops, in addition to delivering materials in library building. Libraries have taken on wide-ranging new linking roles. They are making links from sources of citation to many available sources of content. They are making connections between different library provided resources, and from references found in Internet searches to library provided materials. The new linking role is providing pathways to available information from new locations, taking library services to where users work online, to course software, web browser tool bars, as well as Amazon, Google and other web searches.

Libraries have much to be proud of in the way they have taken on new roles and expanded services to their users. However, our current methods of delivering information are not central to the library's basic role. They are simply a way station in our ongoing search for the best means of serving our users needs and moving toward providing universal discovery and access. The current library environment has developed quite by accident. Until the 1990s, libraries provided only very limited and fragmented access to the available books, serials and other materials. Complete and comprehensive discovery was not technologically or economically possible. The library catalogue provided access to materials in each local library or a regional library consortium. Indexing and abstracting volumes covered subject focused subsets of the world's journal literature. These limited tools were all that was available. Only the largest research libraries could afford all available indexing and abstracting tools, much less the large collections of serial titles indexed by them. There remained large amounts of journal content and vast amounts of other content that were not covered by common indexing tools. Libraries' success in fulfilling their role of providing universal access, and their role in integrating information sources was strictly limited by their economic resources and by the available technology. When libraries had only paper indexes, the local library catalogue and later CD-ROM disks to work with, the limited and fragmented silo information environment that we made available to our users was the result of those limitations. There was not the technological means to tie the materials held in libraries together with the sources in indexing and abstracting tools or the limited full-text content available.

The coming of the World Wide Web in the 1990s began to remove many of the technological restrictions on library's capabilities. Library catalogues developed networked interfaces. It became possible to discover the holdings of most libraries around the world. Indexing and abstracting of ever-larger bodies of serials material moved first to online products and then increasingly to the public Internet. Much more complete coverage of the available literature began to become available. Of course, the online content environment has become vast if not yet universal. There will continue to be substantial economic, organisational and inertial reasons why access is not universal, but most technological reasons for a fragmented information environment, and barriers to integrated access have largely been removed.

The current library content environment has been developed without a great deal of planning. It is largely a conversion of the former paper indexing and abstracting sources, reference sources and paper serials to online versions, with little basic redesign. Database vendors and content providers have created useful products. So far, the movement from paper to online materials has been very cost effective. Online journal content has become available at a substantially lower cost per journal than the paper alternatives. Libraries have made decisions based on subject need, but also based on economics, about the mix of materials they will provide. Journal publishers have individually created access interfaces for electronic versions of their materials. Libraries have often been presented with electronic versions of popular serials and reference materials. As publishers and vendors develop new online products, these materials have been added more or less piecemeal into library collections. Our collections have become richer and broader as a result, but they have also become increasingly complex and ultimately dysfunctional. Library holdings have become more fragmented not less with the addition of online materials.

Tools such as link resolvers and federated search engines are helping to simplify online resources. However, they cannot entirely solve problems of our fragmented information environment. They also add their own level of complexity to the information environment, and as they only mask the fragmented nature of our many individual content silos, they can make the dysfunction of the information environment worse.

Having greatly expanded our offerings and taken on many new online roles, many libraries are returning to their basic integrating role. With new tools available and former technological barriers removed, libraries can make new progress toward the goal of providing unified access to all information.

2.4 The hybrid library

While the Internet and Google lead us to focus on a more unified environment for electronic materials, the integrating role of the library goes beyond providing uniform access to electronic content. Books and other paper materials continue to be a thriving information resource in most libraries. The role of libraries must be to provide seamless access to both historical and modern paper materials, as well as online materials, not to mention freely available Internet resources and pay per use content. Andrew Pace has a bullet on one of his recent presentations that says simply "Get rid of the e"(Pace, 2004), pointing out the need to move beyond having separate systems, services and interfaces for e-content and paper content.

Users need a common body of content that they can easily search and access. Materials managers are also seeking common ways to keep track of content, regardless of format, to make sure that resources are in all the places where users look for them. In the last few years, it has become common to speak about the hybrid library. That is, a library that offers the broad range of paper and electronic, owned as well as accessed, materials. Such a library provides integrated discovery services for its hybrid collection of materials so that the library user can be directed to material without taking any account of whether the material is in print form, or online, or whether it is free or paid material, owned by the local library or delivered from another source.

In a 1998 white paper, Stephen Pinfield, Jonathan Eaton, Catherine Edwards, Rosemary Russell, Astrid Wissenburg, Peter Wynne described the hybrid library as follows.

> The hybrid library is on the continuum between the conventional and digital library, where electronic and paper-based information sources are used alongside each other. The challenge associated with the management of the hybrid library is to encourage end-user resource discovery and information use, in a variety of formats and from a number of local and remote sources, in a seamlessly integrated way. The hybrid library should be "designed to bring a range of technologies from different sources together in the context of a working library, and also to begin to explore integrated systems and services in both the electronic and print environments". The hybrid library should not, then, be seen as nothing more than an

uneasy transitional phase between the conventional library and digital library but, rather, as a worthwhile model in its own right, which can be usefully developed and improved. (Pinfield et al., 1998)

The integration of multiple formats has become a basic and integral part of today's library. Still, the notion of the hybrid library is useful. Integrating traditional paper collections and electronic collections into a seamless whole for library users is an essential and often difficult task. With many libraries still working to include older paper collections in library catalogues, and struggling to include all electronic collections, this is not yet a task that libraries have completed successfully.

3

The library catalogue and the new role of distributed electronic content tools

The library catalogue has long been at the centre of library services. The debate over its shortcomings is equally long standing. Concern about both the functionality of OPACs and the sustainability of cataloguing methods is reaching new levels. Karen Calhoun of the Library of Congress voiced a common concern where she stated, "Today, a large and growing number of students and scholars routinely bypass library catalogues in favour of other discovery tools, and the catalogue represents a shrinking proportion of the universe of scholarly information" (Calhoun, 2006). Despite growing concerns, ILSs continue to be at the centre of library materials management, and the OPAC continues to be the primary public search tool. This is not likely to change. Still, we must address the fact that although our ILSs were once the only tool for managing and accessing library materials, they are now just one of many systems involved in library processes. The range of systems involved in the management, control and delivery of e-materials is greater than ever before. In the last 5 years alone, several new systems have become central to e-content management. These systems operate independently of the Library ILS database. They perform essential services not carried out by the ILS. In some cases, they replace or duplicate some functions of the ILS.

All of these systems are involved in one way or another with integrating the information sources libraries provide. The following is by no means an exhaustive list of systems that are important in the integration of and management of electronic materials. However, it is useful to consider some of the systems involved, and the many ways in which they interact.

3.1 Link resolvers and the knowledgebase

Link resolving, based on the OpenURL standard (NISO, 2005) is the first new materials management technology that has had a profound impact on library services and how ILSs are used. The idea of link resolving is simple. A link resolver is a database that lists all e-journals and other electronic content a library can provide full-text access to. Journal index databases and other search tools that support link resolving place a button in each citation on search results lists they display. Clicking on this button gives the searcher a display showing if the cited material is available in full text in their library, and provides a link to that full text if it is available. Link resolver software is available from a dozen vendors now. Ex Libris SFX, Ebsco LinkSource, and OCLC 1Cate are a few of the more popular link resolvers.

There are also open source link resolvers such as the CUFTS resolver developed for the Council of Prairie and Pacific University Libraries (COPPUL), in Western Canada (Stranack, 2006).

The idea of providing a path from index references to available full text has moved the procession toward a unified information environment, and one-stop shopping, many steps closer. In only about 5 years, nearly all electronic journal and other online content providers have built connections and support for link resolvers into their online interfaces. Major electronic content providers such as Ebsco, Proquest and Gale offer extensive support for many link resolving software applications. Smaller online publishers offer less extensive support for link resolving. There are still electronic content products that do not feature link resolver support at all. However, in just about any search interface our library users might use, they will see a link button in the list of results that will lead them to full text whenever it is available from their library.

Link resolving means that database searchers no longer need to distinguish between table of contents databases, indexing and abstracting databases, or full-text databases. They do not need to concern themselves with the array of electronic content products their library offers. They can treat all library search tools as full text as they will find a link to any available full text from any source they search. A number of web-based journal indexes and document delivery services including Ingenta and MetaPress are bringing the convenience of link resolving to web searching, by providing users with connections to the link resolver of their local library. In the same way link resolver companies have made arrangements with Google so that users identified by IP number as coming from a particular library, university, or other institution get linked from references found in Google web searches, to full text available from content sources available at their local library. OCLC has also added a registry of link resolvers to the Open WorldCat web service. This means that searchers on the Internet can be linked from journals found in the Open WorldCat library catalogue back to the users' local library holdings, using their local library's link resolver.

At the core of a link resolver is a web-accessible database, a "knowledgebase". The knowledgebase contains a record of all electronic journal materials a particular library has access to, with URL links to where full text of that material can be found. One of the most important features of link resolving technology from the materials management perspective is that the link resolver companies have primary responsibility for maintaining and updating the metadata in the knowledgebase. e-Journal content vendors provide the link resolver companies with ongoing information about the e-journals they provide in each database product or e-content package. As Proquest adds and removes content from their ABI Inform aggregated database, or Elsevier adds or removes titles from ScienceDirect, they provide coverage information to the link resolver companies showing the changes to the volumes and issues that are available. This information changes frequently, as vendors add new journals or remove journals from databases. Years of coverage also change frequently. Link resolvers represent a new materials management partnership between electronic content producers, the link resolver company, and libraries.

Another key management feature of link resolvers is that they can provide libraries with reports of changes to the e-journal content they receive from hundreds of different electronic content sources that they have available. Even though all link resolvers must maintain up to date information about changes electronic content packages, at present not all link resolver companies can provide reports of these changes to libraries. Without them, libraries must undertake the difficult and time-consuming task of tracking changes to many electronic content sources individual. Link resolvers that provide information about changing electronic content provide an essential service for libraries to keep an up to date record of their electronic holdings, and manage this information in their ILSs. Some link resolver companies take this role a step further and provide MARC records for journals that can be uploaded to library ILSs to keep journal information up to date.

Link resolvers provide article level linking. That is to say, they make a connection from an individual article citation to the volume, issue and page location for the full text of that article in a web-accessible online product database. Link resolvers duplicate serials holding information that many libraries manually maintain in their ILSs. They automatically update this information, using vendor-supplied information, as e-content changes. Libraries that choose to maintain serials content in the OPAC struggle to keep up with the information being provided in the link resolver. Of course, the link resolvers' capabilities to mine serials holding, volume and issue information, to make connections from references to individual full-text articles go well beyond the capabilities of library OPACs that may contain the same information. Link resolvers also commonly offer a simple A-to-Z journal title search interface for looking up electronic journals offered by a library. A growing number of libraries are relying on their link resolvers rather than on the ILS to keep a record of their serials holdings, and to provide their users with the means to see what serials they have available. Link resolvers are highly adaptable and configurable tools. They are beginning to take on the role of providing linking information for e-books, just as they have for electronic serials. Therefore, they will provide an increasing amount of information that is duplicated in library ILSs.

Many libraries add extensive information about paper serials holdings and other local holdings to their knowledgebase. To get the most out of link resolving, it is necessary for libraries to invest considerable time and effort in adding local content and reviewing the vendor supplied information provided by a knowledgebase. Link resolvers have been a major step forward in making online materials easily accessible, and they will doubtless continue to develop new capabilities.

3.2 Federated searching

Like link resolvers, federated search tools have caused great changes to library services in a very short period (Figure 3.1). These software applications present a common online search interface. They allow the searcher to select from a wide range of individual content databases. They then broadcast the users' search request to each of the selected databases. They receive, merge and sort the results from each search, and display a single result set to the user. The ability to search many online resources with a single search is compelling. Early in the development of federated searching, this was described as "Google-like" searching. The products on the market use names like SingleSearch, CentralSearch, WebFeat, Muse Global and Ex Libris MetaLib, but there are now many federated search applications available. There is general agreement that so far federated search offers limited and basic search capabilities (Webster, 2007b). Each online product has its own methods of indexing and arranging information. Wilson online products offer different search features and capabilities than OCLC First Search products. Subject specific databases in particular may offer indexing features that are specific to each database. A federated search product cannot access all the functionality of each native interface. The detailed and specialised search features of library OPACs also cannot be duplicated by federated search software as yet.

Figure 3.1   **Federated search**

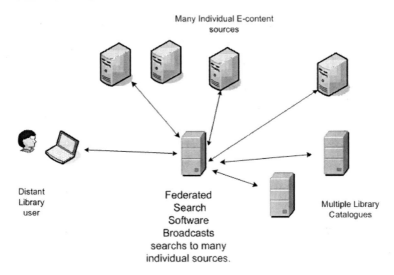

As their features improve, federated search tools have the obvious potential to replace many independent search interfaces, including the library OPAC. The ability to simultaneously search many different sources of information makes it possible to decentralise the storage of electronic content and metadata in many different repositories. It calls into question the basic library practice of attempting to centralise all descriptive metadata in a single ILS. Many libraries are moving away from using many individual proprietary interfaces including the library OPAC. They are increasingly using multiple search applications, in different combinations, as the primary search interfaces for searching library catalogues and other online resources. There are immediate opportunities for OPAC interfaces to develop more federated search capabilities of their own, so that ILSs and link resolvers and other resources, might be searched as one. The possibilities for different combinations of federated search are great. It is no longer necessary to think in terms of one single repository. Libraries should be embracing a future where many resources are searched by a few common interfaces, and working to bring this future about as rapidly as possible.

3.3 Electronic resource management

ERM systems are another important addition to online materials management (Koppel, 2006). They are online database systems intended for integrating all of the information used to management electronic resources, and storing that information in a central location. A wide range of information about electronic content can be stored, including listings of the electronic packages that a library holds, the serials titles contained in those packages, electronic package licence terms and access restrictions, provider service contact phone numbers and e-mail, as well as URLs to access package functions and administration and electronic content access passwords. ERM systems also provide a repository for database usage statistics. There is no question that these online tools present valuable solutions to some of the problems presented by electronic resources. These systems provide a means of collecting important information about electronic materials that cannot be stored in a conventional ILS. ERM systems are carefully linked to link resolver systems. Information about online database title holdings is accessed from the link resolver knowledgebase rather than duplicated in yet another repository. ERM systems can also be extensively linked to some ILSs. Therefore, the additional information they provide about online materials can be accessed and displayed from the library OPAC. ILS vendors and other companies have developed ERM systems. Many of the

ERM vendors, including Innovative Interfaces, ExLibris and Serials Solutions, also offer link resolver applications. ERM systems are based on the ERM specification developed by the Digital Library Federation in the USA after an extensive assessment of the information collection needs and practices of libraries' managing electronic resources (Jewell *et al.*, 2004).

ERM systems provide the database tools for collecting information about electronic resources held by libraries. They provide a means for libraries to gather and centralise this information. However, so far they do not provide enough assistance in collecting that information. They create a new group of largely manual management tasks requiring large amounts of staff time and effort to collect, input and maintain information. ERM systems are linked closely with link resolvers. The content vendors supply much of the information that populates link resolvers automatically. This is one of their most useful features for libraries. ERM systems are built around the same vendor supplied knowledgebases. For systems to be fully successful they must develop methods for automating the passage for information into the ERM system and the library ILS from e-content publishers and vendors.

ERM system vendors are working together on the Standardized Usage Statistics Harvesting Initiative (SUSHI) to develop means for ERM systems to interact with e-content producers to collect usage statistics automatically from multiple database providers. There are also efforts like the Onyx for Serials initiative to exchange serialsubscription information (Miller *et al.*, 2005). The NISO License Expression Working Group is also working on standardisation and automated exchange of licence terms and access rights information (NISO, 2007). As ERM systems become populated automatically with vendor-supplied information, they will be a much greater advance for library materials management than they have been so far. Creating new information collection processes for rapidly growing electronic collections without providing streamlined and automated methods for carrying out those processes is unsustainable, given existing library resources. The real value of ERM systems will be limited as long as they remain databases to be populated, updated and maintained using largely manual methods.

3.4 Document delivery patron services

The network environment has not only made access to large amounts of full-text content possible, it has also greatly facilitated the exchange of materials between libraries. Highly automated document delivery systems allow us to integrate document borrowing from other libraries into the user search experience. Libraries are seeking to integrate access to online and paper materials so that users are routed to the materials they need, regardless of its format. They are also integrating access to material that they do not own, but which can quickly be delivered by other libraries or document delivery providers.

In my own region of Canada, the Council of Atlantic University Libraries (CAUL) is rapidly developing a high-speed document delivery system between academic libraries in the four Canadian provinces of New Brunswick, Nova Scotia, Prince Edward Island, and Newfoundland and Labrador. Users can search for materials in all the participating libraries using federated search software. The users determine local availability using a link resolver. If a loan is needed, users are authenticated for borrowing by their local library ILS. Then, a borrowing request is generated for them by the Relais online Document Delivery software. Four separate online systems, federated search, library OPAC/ILS, link resolver and document delivery, must interact to offer the user this seamless search and retrieval process. Document delivery applications such as VDX and Relais are greatly expanding the materials libraries can offer their users. The information exchange requirements of these document delivery services are becoming an important consideration for ILSs and other systems they need to interact with.

3.5 Citation management

There are a number of citation management applications being used in libraries, including EndNote, ProCite and Refworks. These applications are growing in importance, particularly in academic libraries. They allow researchers to store lists of reference citations to materials they have located online. Many serials databases and other online content sources provide built-in methods for transferring references found in a content source into citation management applications. The primary purpose of citation management applications is to produce bibliographies and citation lists of sources in a wide range of standard academic citation formats, such as Modern Language Association (MLA) or American Psychological Association (APA) style. They automate the process of producing scholarly notes and bibliographies for academic research papers, theses, or other publications.

These products have been available as local software, loaded on individual researchers PCs. But they are now becoming online web-accessible applications. To work effectively these products need to interact with any research database that a scholar might be searching for information. They must be able to receive information from all of the different search interfaces that researchers use, including the library OPAC, federated search applications and link resolvers. As the automated movement of information between many online content sources becomes more important, citation management applications are at the forefront in developing processes for doing this. Citation management applications are also one of a growing number of web applications that allow each individual user to store research information, a record of the searches they have used or the material they have located in ongoing research. Library OPACs and many online journal database interfaces provide personalised user research spaces and customised citation management features. These separate tools should be another target for our integration efforts.

3.6 Proxy servers

In North America, proxy servers are the primary method of authenticating users of library online resources (Webster, 2002). In the UK in particular, the Athens authentication system is typically used instead of proxy servers. But many UK libraries use both a proxy server and Athens. Other methods of authenticating library users, such as virtual private networking, are also used by larger institutional libraries. Newer methods such as Shibboleth and other federated authentication systems may soon replace proxy serving (Shibboleth Project, 2007). But, at present proxy servers are an essential part of many libraries' online access services. They take advantage of widely-used IP authentication. Online content databases check the Internet address (Internet Protocol (IP) number) of computers attempting to log on to access their resources. They permit access only to computers that have IP numbers that belong to a library that is licensed to provide that online product, or to the university or other institution that library is part of. A proxy server acts as an intermediary between users remote from the library and IP authenticated library resources. Proxy servers were created to allow users outside the library to provide a username and password of some sort and then be permitted access to the wide range of services offered in the library. In recent years we have discovered that we can use the proxy not only to provide access to electronic content databases, but also to validate access to federated search services, document delivery services, citation management services, or to any other service restricted to library users.

Most online content databases and many online services have their own means of providing validation other than IP validation. They allow lists of usernames and passwords to be setup, and they can authenticate users in a variety of other ways. Many smaller libraries with a limited number of online resources to offer simply use the internal validation tools offered by each online resource. But maintaining many different lists of passwords is a time-consuming management task. The tools available to provide remote access are different from online service to online service. There are still too many online content products that have very limited internal user authentication; these are effectively unavailable to remote library users without a proxy server. A proxy server acts as a centralising and integrating tool to make one validation process work for many databases (Figure 3.2).

EzProxy is one of the most popular software tools for

Figure 3.2 Proxy server acts as intermediary between remote library users and each IP-validated e-content source

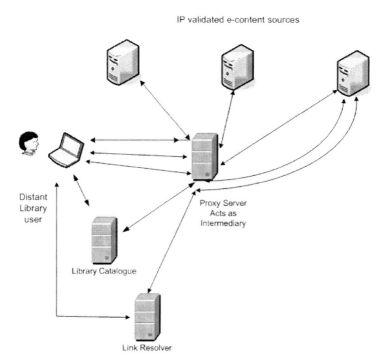

IP validated e-content sources

Distant Library user

Proxy Server Acts as Intermediary

Library Catalogue

Link Resolver

proxying (Zagar, 2007). Several thousand libraries around the world use this proxy software. Not only does it provide central access to many tools, but it will also look for authentication to several sources. It can employ the NCIP protocol to check a library card barcode number and personal identification number (PIN) on an ILS. Or it can be given an e-mail username and password and pass this to an e-mail server to be validated. It can also take a university student ID number and check this against a campus information system, using the standard LDAP database authentication protocol, used by most student information systems, including the Windows LAN networks used on most college and university campuses.

EzProxy does not allow access to just any online product that it is asked to proxy. For security reasons EzProxy software must be configured to act as an intermediary only for specific online resources. Each library must configure the proxy server with a detailed list of URLs for products that it wishes to provide access to. Therefore, the proxy server becomes another place where each library must maintain a list of all available e-resources. Many libraries provide proxy server access to many individual e-journals and electronic resources that they make available, in addition to large databases and electronic content packages. It is possible to maintain lists of many thousands of online resources that an individual library can offer its users. Several libraries have come up with innovative automated processes for adding and removing e-journal entries from EzProxy configuration files on a regular basis (Biles, 2006). Many other libraries have simple restricted access to their OPAC, so that all OPAC users must "log on" or be authenticated by the proxy server. In this way, e-books and e-journals that are only available to authenticated users can be made available through the library catalogue, as only valid users can access the library OPAC. Libraries that do this typically provide guest access to a version of their OPAC that will not provide access to licensed electronic content. Accessing online resources via a proxy server is a simple matter. Each universal resource locator (URL) or an online resource is modified by adding the URL for the proxy server. A prepend URL for the proxy server is added to the URL for each desired online resource. This means that libraries that use proxy servers must amend many thousands of URLs on their websites or portal and in the ILSs that they wish to have authenticated by their proxy server.

Enabling of remote access to licensed materials is now a

fundamental role for libraries. Therefore authentication of valid users is a critical issue that all libraries are addressing. The use of proxy servers has been very successful. Although it is a significant new management task for libraries, it is not difficult for libraries with reasonable resources to manage. If validation is handled well, users can search and access materials in a simple and seamless way. But in such a complex environment where many different resources and service require validation, it is all too easy to end up confronting users with multiple and repeated logins to gain access to different services. Proxy servers play a key role in assisting libraries in providing a well-integrated "single sign on" service.

3.7 Enhanced content services

Enhanced content in the library catalogue is another service that has become important in the last few years. Book cover images add visual appeal to library catalogues. Tables of contents, book descriptions and author information all give the user important additional information with which to select the right book. This extra content provides searchers with additional detail on the topics covered in books but not provided by library catalogue subject headings. Searchable enhanced content adds new dimensions to library catalogues. Syndetics Solutions has provided libraries with different packages of enhanced content. Book agents such as Blackwell also provide table of contents information and publishers are making additional information available as well. Enhanced content metadata can be added to ILSs, record by record, or by batch loading. It can also be linked to from a metadata vendor's servers. Amazon has taken an open and expansive attitude to allowing the book information they collect to be used by other agencies. The company sets requirements and restrictions for the use of its web services, but is encouraging the widest possible distribution of their information. Book cover images, customer reviews and other services from Amazon are being used by some libraries to provide free enhanced content in their library catalogues.

3.8 Social networking tools and resources

From a library perspective, the Internet is not only a means for delivering information. It is also a vehicle for communication and collaboration. The Internet is demonstrating the power of the group, in a variety of new ways. Wikis, web logs (blogs), collective repositories such as the photograph repository Flickr, tagging services such as Del.icio.us, and collective reviewing tools such as Amazon's customer review system have made the Internet highly interactive. They are creating very useful repositories of collaborative and collective information. Libraries are beginning to use collaborative tools such as subject tagging and patron reviews to allow library users to share information, opinion and comment. They are starting to explore the real possibilities of turning library catalogues and portals into interactive community resources, rather than one-way communication tools that only pass information from the library to users. Interactive resources present libraries with a number of new types of collective content and metadata, which will have to be managed in new ways.

3.9 New and additional distributed content tools

There are many other systems and services that could be added to the list of distributed content tools, web-based services, vendor provided systems, or classroom content systems. We can expect that new resources will become important in the coming years. We must plan our information management tools to be flexible and responsive to new developments. Each electronic content tool, including the ILS, should not be thought of as a stand alone, or single purpose application. They are multiuse highly interconnected services that must be built to interact with one another and exchange information in a wide variety of ways.

4

Electronic content products – materials management and integration

In addition to the many online tools involved in content management, e-content products themselves have important materials management features. A growing portion of library materials management efforts go into working with individual electronic content products. These come in a wide range of shapes and sizes, each with strengths, individual service capabilities and management headaches for libraries.

Electronic serials have been the largest part of electronic library collections and the primary focus of electronic materials management. Reference collections are now transitioning quickly from paper to electronic materials. After a slow start, e-book collections are growing in importance. Many reference works are becoming available exclusively in electronic form. In an increasing number of cases, my library is obliged to convert paper versions of handbooks, directories and encyclopaedias to electronic versions, as publishers migrate these works to online only. A great range of government and administrative material has moved from paper depositories in the library to exclusively online materials. Many kinds of local online depositories are also growing in size and prominence. These include materials from statistical datasets to "learning objects" (Shank, 2005) to audio files and images of many kinds. Libraries are increasingly participating in regional and larger online archives, as well as many kinds of e-publishing.

Many of the issues libraries are first encountering with electronic serials will be equally important issues with other kinds of materials.

4.1 Large aggregated full-text and indexing databases

Large packages of full-text journal content from vendors such as Ebsco, Proquest, Gale and H.W. Wilson are the largest source of electronic content. These packages offer full-text content fixed with indexing and abstracting. These generalised packages offer no fixed body of content. The consequence is that availability of journal titles is irregular and, in addition, volume and issue coverage changes frequently. It has also become common for some vendors to embargo the most recent year or 2 years of journal coverage in an attempt to discourage libraries from cutting current paper journal subscriptions. Omnibus packages such as Ebsco Academic or Proquest General Reference are a cost-effective way of providing a large amount of full text. Their embargos are not popular, and their mix of full text along with indexing and abstracting services is confusing for library users. However, the far-reaching coverage of these packages makes them very popular with library users.

The major aggregate services tend to have the most highly developed linking and materials management services. They provide services for linking to Library ILSs and link resolvers and these services offer automatic connections to a library proxy server where one is available. They have well-developed services for responding to search requests from federated search tools. The large aggregators maintain extensive information about the journal holdings in content packages from other major e-content vendors. They also have well-developed systems to allow references found in their search results to be easily cross-linked to full-text content available from other vendors.

The major e-journal content vendors provide internal linking. This is a system where the local library administrator indicates which other e-journal packages they subscribe to. Each aggregator service provides administrative tools for libraries to manage information about which full-text content packages they have available for their users to link to. The e-journal interface will then display a link button on all search results lists, connecting to all available full-text content. Therefore, any references found in an Ebsco search that are available in a Proquest database will have a link button if the library has indicated they subscribe to Proquest. Internal linking services will continue to be very important for the many libraries that do not have a separate link resolver.

The e-content aggregators therefore provide the same services internally that are provided by link resolvers. The aggregators must maintain listings of the serials holdings of their own and other content producers' e-journal packages, in the same way that link resolvers maintain this information. They must provide information sufficient to be able to construct article level links to each article held in each e-content database. The aggregator products that offer internal linking must maintain accurate and up-to-date information on a wide selection of common full-text packages. They are duplicating the work done by link resolver companies in collecting the same information.

In addition to providing services for connecting to proxy servers or other external authentication services such as

Athens, aggregator services provide extensive internal authentication services. These include services for constructing lists of users' names and passwords that can access particular packages, features for restricting access to particular library barcode numbers, and services for restricting access only to requests from particular web pages, such as a library portal page. Many libraries cannot afford or do not feel the need for external authentication. When providing user home access, or other database access outside the library, many smaller libraries rely on the internal authentication services provided by each database aggregator.

e-Content aggregators also provide regular, timely and accurate information about changes to their content packages; journal titles added or removed, titles that have changed, journals that have ceased publication or new journals that have started up. For libraries that maintain information about their electronic holdings in their library catalogues, information from vendors is one critical way of keeping track of content changes. Many libraries rely on this information to regularly update e-journal information in their ILSs. Unfortunately, not all aggregators provide easily accessible information about content additions, removals and title changes. Although content aggregators and link resolver companies have systems for sharing this information, there is no centralised repository of information about the changing content in electronic journal packages.

Larger aggregator packages can be extensively customised. They offer literally hundreds of configurable search and access features in order to customise every aspect of the database to the local libraries' needs. The administrative tools of major aggregators such as Proquest and Ebsco can be managed with relatively little training.

These content vendors also provide extensive telephone and e-mail technical support. Early library efforts to offer online full text involved technically specialised UNIX server management, and often required custom programmed computer system development. Development of relatively simple vendor-hosted full-text content services has been a key element in making electronic content widely accessible.

The linking, authentication and content change information services provided by large aggregator services are an essential part of libraries' effort to integrate and provide common access to the online materials they offer. These easy to administer vendor-hosted services set the bar for what libraries should expect from all online content service providers.

4.2 Large publisher full-text databases

Publishers such as Wiley, Elsevier, Springer, Blackwell and Taylor and Francis offer online search and retrieval services for their own online journals and growing collections of online books. Full or substantial access to these databases is typically purchased in the form of complete packages of all of the publisher's titles.

The products of large publishers such as Elsevier's ScienceDirect or Springer Link are very similar to aggregator packages in many ways. Like large aggregator services, they typically have well-developed administrative tools for setting up links to library ILSs and link resolvers. In addition, many have well-developed services for routing to proxy services and additional authentication features. They also usually provide easily accessible information about content changes. Some large publishers provide at least summary MARC record metadata for the e-serials provided in their collections. This is something increasingly provided by aggregator services as well.

However, individual publisher products are focused only on providing access to their own content. They show considerably less interest in integration than aggregator product vendors that specialise in mixed full-text and indexed content from many sources. Their interest in provided good linking services is lower as they provide no indexing information about other vendors' content, which would need links to full text. But, in reality, libraries hold paper copies of journals and books indexed in these sources and may not purchase online full-text access to all materials. Publishers' databases routinely provide index access to materials or product coverage that some libraries will not have full-text access to. Publishers' products often offer recent coverage as one package of material, while offering archive or back file materials at an additional price. They are also increasingly offering e-journal content and e-book content in the same database as separate priced packages. So, in this case, users are presented with index information for material that they do not have full-text access to. Therefore, accessing linking services that will connect users to paper copies of this material, or other sources, are still important. Large publishers are often less aware of their role in the materials management partnership with other e-content providers than aggregator services tend to be.

The large publishers, along with major content aggregators, set the standard for search interface functionality and online content management services. Like large aggregators, these publishers provide information, authentication and other services that are essential to libraries in their effort towards integrating access to many online products.

Just as with link resolving, management of online materials from major publishers and aggregators is also a new kind of partnership between vendors and libraries, with content vendors providing detailed holdings, linking information and management services that libraries can customise to connect services together.

Still, aggregators and publishers are reporting their holdings and changes in different ways to multiple places. Libraries, e-content vendors and link resolver vendors are often duplicating each other's work by separately maintaining holdings and linking information. The current situation would seem to cry out for a coordinated approach with one or more shared public repositories of content and linking information.

4.3 Small publisher websites

Libraries also access many independently subscribed online journals from smaller publishers, which may offer full text of only a few journals via their sites, or may offer collections of dozens or hundreds of publications. Connections to link resolvers or proxy servers, services and other built-in features for integration, individual customisation, or user authentication are often limited or missing on small publishers' sites. These sites may not maintain robust services for connecting to federated search software. The platforms are less frequently updated with improved search and administrative features. Title lists and holdings information for many smaller publishers are not available from all link resolver products. Thus, libraries often have to maintain title lists for these sites in link resolvers manually and do extra work administering the e-content coming from these sites. As integrating services develop and become more essential for libraries, many smaller publishers are struggling to keep up with the latest management services.

4.4 Individual journal webpages

Virtually all journals available on the market now have an individual webpage available. Many journals have several large and extensive websites providing different kinds of information. Popular publications typically have sites specifically devoted to an individual journal, where promotional information about the journal and its content are featured. Sample free full-text content is often available. It is also common to find prepublication copies of upcoming articles online. Freely available indexing of the content from many publishers is also commonly available, in addition to paid full-text access.

It is very common for individual journal sites and publisher sites to provide free searching of indexed online content and its abstracts, in addition to subscribed full-text access. This table of contents indexing and abstracting is typically made available to Google and other web search engines, to be freely available for searching on the World Wide Web. Many scholarly journals also offer subscription access websites, where supplemental materials, supporting data and the like can be seen. Typically, these sites focus on readers who have a particular interest in one periodical. There are individual online subscription versions of popular periodicals, such as *The Economist*, or *Business Week*. These often feature special supplemental material not found in the print publication. These are separate from the online content of journals in aggregator packages or publisher databases, and cater to a different market. It is common for libraries to be provided with access to individual journal web pages, or publisher web pages of promotional and supplemental materials, available to paper and electronic journal subscribers. This leaves libraries with confusing decisions about which websites associated with a journal they should provide access to, and what methods they should use for doing so.

Most libraries work with this wide array of electronic sources on a daily basis. It is important to remember that electronic content sources are not uniform. They provide very different levels of management services. Each application provides different levels of support for linking to other resources and integrating that tool into a common information environment. As libraries work to make the complex electronic content environment as easy as possible for our users to navigate, they need to set clear standards about the integration services require from all online content providers.

The large number of different systems involved in delivering electronic materials has created a substantial new area of materials management work. Each application, and each individual content interface, requires attention and management, to a greater or lesser extent. It is common for individual content providers to maintain metadata in several different repositories that must be accessed separately. So title list information for an online database may be found at one online location, while administrative and configuration information for the same database may be accessed at a different site, and usage statistics at yet another location.

Libraries using these tools are devoting a substantial amount of time to administration. The tasks to perform include checking off e-content packages they subscribe to in each vendor interface so that smart links will appear, setting up different methods of authentication, and/or customising each interface with the library name and logo. These are relatively straightforward management tasks. The management of tools such as link resolvers and federated search applications is more complex, but often feature many of the same tasks.

Much of the work maintaining electronic content applications is repetitive. The same information is maintained in many different systems using different software. URLs, ILSs, proxy servers, lists of accessible holdings, password and other authentication information, lists of authorised IP numbers for each product, library logo and local branding information are among the data elements that must be kept up to date for each source. So far, most of this work must be done individually with each system and interface. There are enormous possibilities for developing services to share administrative preferences and configure all these individual systems using common style sheets or other centralised methods.

5

The ILS and the challenges of electronic materials

Even with the broad selection of systems now involved in providing electronic materials, integrated library systems remain at the centre of library materials management. The growth of electronic materials has greatly changed the demands made on ILSs and cataloguing processes. Although libraries have changed methods a great deal in the last decade, they are continuing to struggle with electronic collections and continuing to rethink approaches to materials management. Karen Calhoun's comment that "the catalogue is in decline, its processes and structures are unsustainable, and change needs to be swift" is a view shared by a growing number of librarians.

Despite major efforts to automate and reduce duplication, cataloguing processes are still too largely manual, and at their core little changed in many decades. They are based on the individual editing of each catalogue record for each item held by the library and the manual assignment of holdings. These processes are now highly computerised. Standardised descriptive metadata is widely shared and copied by many libraries rather than being created from scratch. Nonetheless, the process of manually reviewing, tracking and updating records for each item has remained.

Our manual methods for inputting and editing cataloguing records were devised, and continue to work successfully, for the inventory control of locally-held book and serial paper materials. However, the role of libraries has changed from being owners of locally-held materials to being stewards of widening selections of materials that include paper and electronic materials that they own, electronic materials that are licensed for access, freely available material, and document delivery materials that are ordered on demand. Libraries now act as clearing houses to provide access to collections of materials from many sources.

Bodies of available electronic material have greatly increased the size of most library collections. In the libraries that I am most familiar with, available serials collections have grown three to five times in the last decade. David Kohl and Tom Sanville have suggested that consortium purchasing of electronic materials increased serials collections in OhioLink libraries by four times on average, and by as much as 20 times in some cases (Kohl and Sanville, 2006). The increase in materials can vary a great deal, depending on how libraries chose to handle materials such as open access journals and freely available government documents. e-Book collections may be beginning the same trend. As library staffing is not increasing to the same extent, there is a great deal more material to catalogue without comparable increases in available staffing.

Our workflow and methods were devised at a time when once materials had been put into a library catalogue, there was relatively little need to remove or change record information. This is particularly true of serials. A subscribed periodical might end publication or change title. These changes would have to be manually inserted into the library catalogue. However, once paper volumes were on a library's shelves, it was a rare occurrence that catalogue records for these volumes would need to be substantially altered or need to be removed from the library catalogue.

e-Content collections experience a rate of change that is far greater than the rate of change in owned paper collections. Large volumes of material require URL changes. The amount of material entering and exiting e-content databases is very great. Today library cataloguers face an environment where it is routine for hundreds of journals to move from one vendor to another. New e-journals come and go from e-journal packages frequently. Companies such as Springer, Elsevier and Wiley may create several new journals each year. Journals move from one publisher to another, and journals end publication. Many of the e-journals that libraries licence originate from aggregators that licence content from various publishers. Journal content formerly available from the Ebsco Corporation is now coming from Cambridge Scientific and content formerly available from a publisher's website is now available from the HireWire online interface. It is common for large blocks of e-journal content to move from one vendor to another. Electronic content products commonly have a specific time period for material covered. A library may purchase only the current 10 years, as an example. Therefore, each year, holdings for each electronic journal are reduced by 1 year, while 1 year of new content is added. For the library catalogue to remain up to date, these changes must be reflected in a timely manner.

The amount of change that is taking place in online collections is very different to what our processes were developed for. Large new collections are being added to library holdings as well, through consortium purchases and back file or large e-book acquisitions. Open access materials and other free resources have the potential to expand available materials even further. Even with current automated methods, many libraries are not keeping up with the demands of online materials. Their cataloguing resources are overwhelmed by catalogue management work that must be performed. The amount of material that could be added to library catalogues is outstripping libraries' staffing and computing capacities.

Serials material continues to make up the major portion of electronic materials for most libraries. In a 2003 study, Peter McCracken of Serials Solutions concluded that most libraries are not able to maintain a record of e-serials in their OPAC. Therefore, they are failing to provide catalogue access to large portions of their available journal collections.

The study compared electronic journal holdings versus all journal holdings in 60 institutions in the USA, in each of the Carnegie classifications of Associate institutions, Baccalaureate, and Masters; 30 institutions in the Carnegie classification of Doctorate; and 25 public libraries, and found the following:

> For Associates institutions, on average, 86.5 per cent of their periodical titles are available electronically. For Baccalaureate institutions, on average 83.3 per cent of their periodical titles are available electronically. For Masters institutions, on average 71.3 per cent of their titles are available electronically. For Doctoral institutions, on average 39.5 per cent of their titles are available electronically. For public libraries, on average 64.3 per cent of their titles are available electronically. As almost none of these institutions are tracking their electronic journals through their online catalogues, most academic libraries in the USA are unable to access between 80 per cent and 90 per cent of their

entire periodical collection. They may have an A-to-Z list of their electronic journals, but this requires that patrons know to search both the OPAC and the A-to-Z list when seeking a specific title. Without effective quality control, some A-to-Z lists contain the numerous errors that were initially introduced by the aggregators themselves. Libraries without A-to-Z lists have almost no knowledge of what they can access through their myriad titles.

Electronic journals are a fact of life in today's library. Patrons and librarians recognize their value; and access through database aggregators, while occasionally problematic, is also incredibly cost-effective. Unfortunately, however, the vast majority of most libraries' journal holdings are now compiled within these databases, and very few libraries are able to track the journals in these databases, particularly through the OPAC. If libraries are to obtain the greatest possible value from the journals in these databases, they need to present information about these journals to their patrons. (McCracken, 2003)

The library catalogue has, for decades, been used as a centralised repository for integrating materials. Uniform catalogue records are created for many different collections and types of materials. They can all then be discovered and located with a single search. There is no question that there are advantages to this approach of centrally cataloguing all materials that each library wishes to provide access to. Each library has built a monolithic database of "holdings", largely duplicated with other library collections. This approach has succeeded in providing a sort of one-stop shopping, with a centralised search of large amounts of material. Nevertheless, this approach is now breaking down. The volume of that can be discovered has increased. The frequency of changes to materials covered has increased as well. Many libraries are finding that moving records in and out of the library catalogue a time consuming, technically challenging, and costly means of achieving integration, and in many cases, simply beyond their resources.

As libraries have made the transition away from paper serials, the extra cataloguing work created by electronic serials has been somewhat offset by a decline in the need for various management tasks associated with paper collections. There are fewer binder services to update and fewer serials to cardex. However, the volume of work is continuing to grow. The basic shortcomings in our methods are being more and more exposed.

The centralised, local catalogue approach is proving to be insufficient in a number of ways. The need for accurate, up to date and complete metadata is still at the heart of library materials management. It is, perhaps, more important than ever. In order to search and access a particular online document from a great array of sources and materials, many metadata elements are needed. Library cataloguing methods are able to supply only some of the needed metadata. Library catalogues provide the needed bibliographic description and local holdings information. Notwithstanding, there is much other essential information that cannot be stored in library collections. The ability to provide article level indexing of serials has always been beyond the capabilities of library cataloguing methods. This indexing information must continue to come from vendor sources. Each library also must maintain complete information on the online sources where the needed issue for this publication can be accessed. This must go along with complete information on which sources are available to the individual library, but also available to other libraries and document delivery services that a particular library may have access to.

The centralised catalogue model is being replaced; in many ways has already been replaced by a distributed, cooperative model, where the library ILS is not the sole repository for library collection metadata, or the single interface for user search and retrieval. Each library is not independently responsible for maintaining all information about its holdings. Instead, important metadata is held in several repositories – the ILS being but one. The ILS dynamically exchanges information with other online systems. It links to other metadata repositories for information, and is used as a source of metadata by other online services. Metadata is maintained in a cooperative effort between many libraries, content vendors and publishers. Users have access to numerous search interfaces to search and retrieve materials from a wide selection of content sources, depending on their needs.

I have little doubt ILSs and MARC methods will continue to play a central role in our efforts to provide integrated access to materials. There is still much that works very well with the longstanding library cataloguing model. But it is clear that we must continue to fundamentally redefine cataloguing processes and recognise when existing approaches are unsustainable. We must come to see ILSs as useful tools for controlling one portion of the materials we steward, and only one of several central repositories that make up the basic library search we offer users as a starting point to their information seeking. It will continue to be a difficult task for each individual library to find the balance between maintaining collections in the local library's ILS or to search collections in a distributed way. The advantages of locally cataloguing materials must be weighed against the time and effort and disadvantages of duplicating effort to copy or recreate cataloguing metadata already available from vendors or other sources. It is still important to recognise that a management model that relies on individual editing of library records as changes are needed is not sustainable in the new electronic information environment.

Fortunately, the scope for improving our methods of materials management is very great. The basic library cataloguing practices represent a major duplication of effort, with thousands of libraries around the world duplicating the same MARC records, duplicating endless changes to electronic journal and e-book holding and URL linking information, and individually making manual changes to these records. Bob Nardini, with the book vendor Coutts Information Services, recently pointed out that libraries are purchasing a growing proportion of cataloguing copy as they purchase new books, therefore it is very much in the interests of book vendors as well to streamline and automate the cataloguing process (Nardini, 2007). The Functional Requirements for Bibliographic Records (FRBR) initiative of the International Federation of Library Associations and Institutions (IFLA) provides a new conceptual framework for organising and describing electronic materials (Tillett, 2004). FRBR is being widely discussed, and elements of FRBR are finding their way into some online systems. FRBR principles will be one of the bases for more functional and efficient library systems, but even so, it has not had a wide impact on ILSs and practice. We also have many models, on the World Wide Web and particularly in e-commerce, of more efficient and effective shared and distributed management models to guide us.

5.1 Automated information exchange

Automation of cataloguing processes is one important means of dealing with the growing flood of catalogue maintenance work created by electronic materials. The libraries I work with are coming to rely on the batch loading of large groups of cataloguing records, in addition to search and replace tools for altering or removing groups of records. The batch loading and search and replace tools available in ILSs have become much better in recent years, although they vary a great deal from one ILS to another. Libraries with older ILSs may have very limited or difficult to use batch loading features. Batch or package management of cataloguing records is becoming a prominent part of our information management strategy. Our efforts are increasingly aimed at modifying large groups of records, and finding ways to avoid the time consuming business of visiting each record individually.

Most library systems today were populated by automated means. They were loaded from previous generations of ILSs, with data that was batch loaded into them. Today's ILSs conform to a number of important interoperability standards. Most ILSs are based on the industry standard relational database ORACLE or some other large commercial database. This means that they can be searched using Structured Query Language (SQL), an open and ubiquitous commercial database search standard, which makes it easy to search access and manipulate database contents in a standardised way. Modern ILSs also typically conform to the Lightweight Directory Access Protocol (LDAP) information exchange format, and they conform to the Open DataBase Connectivity standard (ODBC). These are computer-industry-wide protocols designed to provide an easy and standardised means of exchanging information between different online systems and databases. Libraries have been successful at working out many of the variations and inconsistencies in MARC records, making it easier to share metadata between libraries. We have well-developed systems for copy cataloguing and sharing MARC records between libraries, searching for and easily pushing records from one ILS into another. e-Journal vendors and e-book aggregators can often provide MARC records for the journals or e-books included in packages they provide.

Therefore, when libraries purchase a new e-journal database or a collection of e-books they can easily batch load catalogue records for those materials into the ILS. A growing amount of MARC is provided free of additional charge, as part of e-journal and e-book purchases. It is in the interest of libraries to look to publishers to provide MARC records, as well as other online accessible metadata, as a regular part of product support. We have easier access to metadata and better tools than ever before for automating the movement and modification of cataloguing records. The move to more batch management of library catalogue records is an essential step forward, but it is presenting libraries with some interesting problems. It is common to hear of situations in which libraries have painted themselves into corners because of the cataloguing methods they have used. Library ILS databases are an information resource built up through many thousands of hours of labour. Often, each library record has been carefully customised over an extended period. These databases were not structured with automated modifications of large numbers of records in mind.

I was recently discussing a situation in which some 50,000 MARC records need to be replaced with enhanced records supplied by a vendor. The business of batch loading vendor-provided MARC records and enhancements, such as tables of contents, are becoming commonplace. In this case, the 50,000 records had been carefully customised over several years. Replacement with stock vendor records will mean a substantial loss of information. The ILS in question has reasonable search and replace features, nevertheless, it has proved nearly impossible to insert enhanced fields into large numbers of selected records without losing valuable data in existing record fields. As is often the case, the solution proved to be a detailed and difficult database management task that required many hours of programming and a number of test batch-loadings to get right.

The risks of losing cataloguing data are real. In addition, often there are trade-offs to be made between the speed and efficiency of automated search and replace methods or the much slower, and ultimately unsustainable, but exacting process of manual and individual record maintenance.

The increasing use of batch management is having an impact on how library catalogues are structured. As an example, batch loading is easiest if each instance of each book or serial has an entirely separate catalogue record. If there are multiple copies of a book or journal in different formats it is easiest if each copy has an independent catalogue record. Hence, many libraries maintain individual bibliographic records for each instance of books and journal titles. They therefore have individual MARC records for the paper version of each journal, and they have separate records for each electronic version of each journal. It is very common for library electronic collections to have multiple copies of the same journal. This is a well-known problem with electronic collections. Libraries receive electronic material from many aggregators and publishers. Many journals are available from more than one online database. Added to this, there are often multiple copies of the same journal in non-electronic formats. *Time* magazine or *The Economist* are both good examples. These journals are available online from multiple sources. They are also available in paper. Older copies are available in microfilm. Having separate bibliographic records makes it simple to add and remove records as needed, or edit bibliographic records by removing them entirely and replace them with new, amended records. However, it can confront users with possibly dozens of records for the same work, particularly for popular journals.

Many libraries have chosen to have single bibliographic records for each journal title, and simply attach multiple holdings records for each paper or electronic version of the journal; libraries have been doing this long before batch loading of records was common. My provincial academic library consortium has chosen this route. Therefore, in our library catalogue there is one primary record for the journal *The Economist*. Holdings for each instance of the journal in difference formats are then attached to this record. We feel that it is much easier for library users to find a single listing for *The Economist*, with a list of different places you can access it, than to be confronted with multiple entries for *The Economist* and have to figure out which is the copy most useful in a particular situation. By making the decision to merge bibliographic records in this way, we believe that we have made the library catalogue easier to use. Nevertheless, this approach makes the business of making batch changes to catalogue records more difficult. For example, when Springer ceases to offer a group of journals holdings, information for these journals must be removed from the catalogue. This is much more difficult to do if this electronic holdings information is attached to common catalogue entries that also include holding information for other copies of the same journals. Complex changes to holdings,

URL linking and other information must be carefully added and removed from existing records, rather than the simpler process of removing groups of complete MARC records and inserting MARC records. The most up to date ILSs have good customisable search and replace routines. Therefore, specific fields in particular records can be located and updated. But no ILS does this work really well.

Although libraries feel that they have created highly automated library processes over the last few decades, there is much further to go. ILSs were designed largely for the manual input and removal of information. There are great possibilities to restructure these databases so that they more easily accommodate the automated manipulation of large groups of records. However, this sort of management requires an entirely different set of skills than traditional cataloguing skills. The work requires computer database management skills and a level of ILS knowledge and access not possessed by the great majority of library cataloguers. Batch loading and complex programmed group changes to cataloguing records also carry a much higher level of risk than the changing of individual records. Any small error in setting criteria for changing large groups of database records can result in the wrong records being modified or deleted, or the wrong database fields being overwritten. Libraries should be looking to their ILS vendors for better and simpler search and replace and batch management utilities, which put automated catalogue records management in the hands of library cataloguers rather than system administrators, while ensuring the safety of catalogue data.

We have the ability to take the automation of ILS data management much further than batch loading of records and global search and replace. Libraries have a great opportunity to automate the movement of metadata into and out of ILSs. The critical piece largely missing in our evolving systems so far is a much more extensive exchange of metadata between vendors and publisher systems and ILS, link resolvers, ERM and other library systems.

The ability to connect information in global repositories to local library databases is at the heart of emerging new models. New approaches require systems to have robust built-in methods for exchanging information. They need to be designed with the aim of passing information in and getting it out again in an automated way. Libraries need to be actively pursuing automated means of collections metadata in library systems. Looking at web-based systems such as Amazon, and the automated exchange methods we have developed so far, it is very possible to contemplate a library ILS where the great majority of metadata in the catalogue arrives and leaves by machine interaction, rather than human editing of individual records.

Book and e-journal vendors are making large bodies of MARC records readily available, some of which are included in the purchase price of electronic materials. Table of contents information and other enhanced content is also widely available. e-Book and e-journal vendors routinely supply lists of URLs, which can be added to library catalogues for accessing full-text and supplemental content. Serials jobbers such as Ebsco and Blackwell are actively developing online systems, which provide detailed metadata about electronic serials holdings. Therefore, there are large resources available to provide libraries with metadata, but for the most part these resources do not yet provide a means of moving this information directly into library systems.

Link resolvers provide one of the most obvious models for the automated and unmediated movement of vendor provided metadata into library systems. Vendors supply information about serials holdings and changes to serials databases, which is automatically input into individual libraries' knowledgebases managed by the link resolver companies. This model can be applied to many other areas of electronic materials management particularly the library ILS. Electronic resource management systems are intended to provide an automated bridge between the metadata in link resolver knowledgebases and ILSs and make both repositories accessible via library OPAC systems. However, so far methods for unmediated flow of metadata into ILSs are talked about but not widely implemented.

The Onyx for Serials information exchange protocol is being developed to allow standardised methods for moving serials metadata in and out of library systems including ILSs and link resolvers, as well as exchanging information between different vendor systems. Onyx for Serials is building upon the Onyx standard used by book vendors to automate the movement of descriptive metadata about books between different systems (Miller *et al.*, 2005).

Electronic document interchange (EDI) has become a common method for moving book purchasing and invoicing information from book vendor online systems into library systems in an automated way. Like link resolvers, EDI clearly demonstrates the possibilities for vendor-supplied information to be automatically added and removed from library systems. EDI methods can be used for automatically populating library catalogues with MARC information supplied by book vendors, as well as providing invoice and purchasing information. EDI is a very valuable and promising development, but like so many other information exchange standards, EDI is not nearly as completely implemented as it should be. Book vendors support only some ILSs and EDI features and capabilities vary a great deal on different systems. Regardless, this is a good demonstration of the possibilities for automated and cooperative management where data held by vendors can be moved in and out of individual library catalogues with greatly reduced human intervention.

The NCIP protocol was developed to allow the automated exchange of patron and circulation-related information between different library systems. It is another example of the promise of automated information exchange, but again it is a standard that is inconsistently implemented between different systems, and is not as extensively used as it could be.

5.2 Links and link resolving

URLs are fundamental to accessing specific online information on the World Wide Web. The OpenURL standard, which underlies link resolver technology, is proving to a key component in many efforts to link online information systems together and create a better-integrated information environment (Apps and MacIntyre, 2006). The addition of URL links to web-accessible materials has been one of the most important enhancements to library catalogue in recent years. URLs allow library catalogues to provide links to full-text electronic journals and e-books. They also provide links to supplemental information such as tables of contents, author biographies and other information. As large numbers of e-books begin to be added to our library catalogues, the number of possible links to electronic content will increase greatly. To the tens of thousands of e-journal links that many library catalogues already offer, we can expect to add hundreds of thousands of e-book links. This is a very exciting development. As large amounts of e-journal and e-book content become available via URL, library catalogues become much richer and more attractive tools for users. They become full-text access tools.

In users' minds, the utility of a tool that will lead them directly to content is far greater than a tool that gives them only citation information. Indexes perform only one interrupted step in the larger search and retrieval process. We have seen link resolvers transform how users perceive indexing and abstracting databases. These databases were a poor second choice to full-text databases. However, the addition of link resolving allows these tools to lead users directly to available full text. Therefore, indexing and abstracting tools are now more heavily used and better appreciated. The same is happening to library OPACs as they become capable of linking to large amounts of electronic content. Library catalogues become content access tools, rather than simply discovery tools. Linking to full-text content and linking to supplemental information via URL has become a key part of OPAC functionality. The inclusion of many thousands of URLs in today's library catalogues contribute substantially to the workload issues associated with electronic materials. The well-known system used in library catalogues is to put a URL pointing to an electronic resource in the MARC 856 field for each MARC record where an electronic version is available. These 856 fields link to a webpage where an electronic copy of the catalogued item can be accessed or to additional information about the catalogued item available online. In fact, any online book or journal can have several important URLs (for example, links to tables of contents, background or additional information) in addition to multiple locations for full-text content. Often the first challenge is to determine which URLs are useful to link to, and how to distinguish between them. URLs must be kept up to date in not only the ILS but also in other systems such as link resolvers, federated search applications and ERM systems as well.

The wide range of materials to which it is possible to link from library catalogues can present difficulties as Roy Tennant described in a recent study entitled *"Trouble in online paradise: an analysis of MARC 856 usage at one institution"*. This study examined 200,000 URLs in MARC 856 fields in the University of California library catalogue. It found that in a high percentage of cases there is no way of distinguishing a URL leading to supplemental or descriptive material from a link leading to a full-text copy of the catalogued item itself. As Tennant describes it:

> The students and faculty at the University of California have made it clear that they highly value full online access to the items they locate, and I doubt there are many users who would disagree with this opinion. Therefore, it is important to solve the current problems we have with making it easy for our users to both discover this content and easily retrieve it.
>
> As I have outlined here in anecdotal form, our MARC/AACR2 infrastructure and how it has been put into practice within at least one library is preventing us from effectively fulfilling these valid user needs. For the short term, I believe there are some strategies that can provide a decent solution to these issues for the bulk of our material. But going forward, we need to find and implement an unambiguous, machine-processable method to specify when a URL will fetch the complete item. We cannot allow optional local practices to continue to be the basis upon which we rest our solutions. (Tennant, 2007)

This is just one of many examples where with current practices, the library catalogue is not providing the information needed for effective integration with online content.

There are several standards for persistent URLs (PURL), or Digital Object Identifiers (DOI). The idea behind persistent URLs is to provide URLs to electronic content that remain consistent over time despite changes in the online environment. If the details of an e-journal's location change, the name of its server, its domain name, or the e-journal's location on the vendor's server changes, the URL to that journal should not be changed. In theory, even if an e-journal moves from one publisher to another, a well-constructed persistent URLs should not change. Persistent URLs are commonly used whenever possible in library catalogues. Therefore, the URLs in 856 fields are not supposed to change frequently. In practice, however, we find that URLs in 856 fields change all the time. Some materials in library catalogues such as freely available material do not use persistent URLs. Links to this material frequently become out of date or broken. Also, both Ebsco and Proquest have changed their methods of creating URLs in the last several years. This has required all persistent URLs to electronic journals provided by these vendors to be altered. Changes of this kind result in hundreds or thousands of 856 field changes. Automated search and replace methods are essential in this kind of work.

5.3 Link checking

Library catalogues are coming to have many thousands of URL links in them. We are confronted with the growing task of link checking to keep URLs up to date and working.

Despite the use of persistent URLs, substantial numbers of broken URLs are inevitable.

It is common for modern ILSs to have good automated link-checking software. Of course, there are many libraries using older or very basic ILSs, where link-checking capabilities are limited. Link checking at its best can only check each URL and provide a report about all links, which fail to return a webpage, or return an error message. Link-checking software cannot help with links that continue to work, but now show an out-of-date or superseded webpage. My library users routinely notify me of URL links, which return a webpage that says, "The resource you are looking for has been moved to the following new URL", or "The resource you are looking for has not been found". As these links continue to return a working webpage, automated link resolving does not help with discovering them. Once link checking identifies a lengthy list of URLs that are no longer working, it is then a human task to investigate each error, attempt to locate a new or alternate URL, and decide to fix or remove a link. The more links in our catalogues there are, the more users come to rely on them and then expect and require that links be kept up to date and working. A recent study found that only 35 per cent of libraries do any sort of link checking. They found that of the surveyed libraries that were able to check for dead links, none were checking for changed or relocated linked materials (Burke *et al.*, 2003). Although automated link checking is straightforward for many ILSs, link maintenance and repair is a difficult and time-consuming task that a growing number of libraries are finding it difficult or impossible to keep up with.

Linking to full-text sources and additional information from the library catalogue is a very popular feature. It is one of the advances bringing new credibility to the library OPAC. Nevertheless, it is a service that will prove more and more unsustainable without automated methods and new approaches to exchanging URL information between vendors and library systems.

There is no easy solution to the challenges of linking from library catalogues. Libraries must do everything they can to support the use of persistent URLs that remain unchanged, despite changes to the host systems where electronic content is stored.

We should be routinely speaking up when major vendors move large amounts of material or change large numbers of URLs. The web service Crossref has shown the possibilities for a global, cooperatively publisher managed URL linking repository. Crossref is not sufficiently complete or authoritative yet to become to the sole repository for linking URLs, but it clearly demonstrates the possibility. Libraries should be supporting Crossref and services like it and in addition, encouraging our electronic content suppliers to contribute information about their materials to this and other central repository efforts. When Crossref becomes more complete and accurate, then repositories with URL links to all electronic materials libraries will be able to look to this central source as a primary authority for URLs.

Even with the most efficient automated methods, inserting and maintaining great numbers of URLs in the library catalogue is a fundamentally inefficient practice. Libraries need to be working toward new methods, which rely on linking to URLs stored outside individual library catalogues, and managed by vendors, publishers and serials agents, rather than by individual libraries. Many libraries are moving away from keeping URLs in their ILSs. Instead, they are linking all 856 fields to their link resolver. Several libraries in my regional consortium, including my own, are moving to replace unique URLs in all electronic serials records with a standard URL that calls the library's link resolver. The only unique part of each link resolver URL is the ISSN number of the serial being called. When a link is selected in the catalogue, the link resolver then provides the needed link to the e-content being requested. These 856 fields should only need to be altered if the location of our link resolver changes. The link resolver contains URLs to the online site location for each e-journal. These URLs may change frequently. However, they are updated and maintained largely by the link resolver company, not the library. We are convinced that this distributed approach will save a great deal of library staff time, and may be the only practical way we can maintain the growing number of URL linked to by our catalogue.

5.4 Linking, authentication and remote access

Providing access to online library resources from outside library buildings or from off-campus, for example, direct from users' homes and offices, is a critical component of library services today. In many libraries, remote access to online services exceeds local usage. Making links to e-materials work effectively for remote library users is another challenge. Proxy servers are very common and useful tools for providing remote access to library services, but they add a level of complexity to the process. IP validation is central to most library content licensing. Libraries supply lists of their IP numbers to database vendors. It is very common for libraries to route all URLs that call databases via library proxy servers. The URLs used to call databases from a library webpage actually contain the web address of the library's proxy server. When a user clicks on a link to a database on a library webpage

(Proquest, for example), the link will route them to the library proxy server first. The proxy server then checks their IP number. It will hand the transaction directly to Proquest and take no further action if the user's IP number allows them to access the database. The proxy server will allow direct database access to computers in the library building or on the library's associated campus. If the user's IP number indicated that the computer is not in the library or on campus, then the proxy server will ask the user to log on with authenticating information such as a library ID and password. The proxy server then acts as an intermediary in the transaction between the user's computer and Proquest's server (Figure 5.1).

Figure 5.1 **Linking the library catalogue to e-content proxy service**

Option 1. User is authenticated by the proxy server after library catalogue search. No library catalogue login is required. Validation is required to access each individual e-content resource.

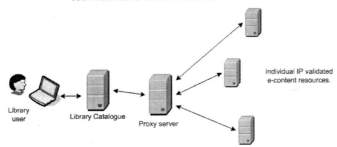

Option 2. User is authenticated by the proxy server before accessing library catalogue. A logon to the library catalogue is required. No further validation is needed to access e-content resources.

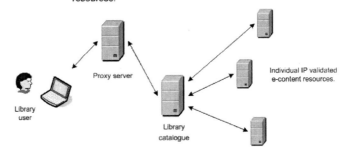

The proxy server approach has been very successful for the libraries using it. However, it does require the extra management of all URLs that link to IP-validated electronic content resources. Each URL to be validated for remote users must have the proxy server's URL added to its beginning, or prepended to it. Any change to the library's proxy server address requires a change to all URLs that use that address.

The URL links in 856 fields in library catalogues also need to work effectively for remote users. Many of these links also lead to electronic content that is validated by the IP number of the user's computer. Without the intervention of a proxy server, only computers within the library or its associated college or university campus are authorised to use that IP-validated resources. The computers of remote users do not have authorised IP addresses, so they will be denied access to IP authenticated sources.

There are two ways to overcome this problem using a proxy server. Remote users can be directed to the proxy server and authenticated before they use the library catalogue. In this case, users are presented with a login screen that asks for their library card number and a password, or some other ID, such as a university ID. Once a user is authenticated in this manner, the proxy server provides access to restricted materials. Once authenticated, library catalogue users may view e-books or connect to electronic journal holdings linked through the library catalogue without an additional log in. The difficulty with this approach is that users without an ID cannot view the library catalogue. In this case, users may be presented with the two ways to access the library catalogue; one that requires a user login, and a second "guest" catalogue link that does not require a login, but that denies remote users access to full-text links. The second approach is to begin each URL in each 856 field in the library catalogue with a call to the library's proxy server. Each URL now calls the proxy server rather than an e-content database directly. The proxy server knows to ask only remote users for validation, and if validation is successful, then to pass traffic on to the specified e-content database. The result of using proxy prepends on links to full text, is that remote users do not need to log on to the library OPAC. There is no confusion between guest users and validated users. Only when and if remote users select a link to a full-text resource will the user be presented with a login screen. Many libraries prefer the openness and simplicity of this approach. Its downside is that there are large numbers of proxy prepended URLs to be managed in the library catalogue. Any change to the location or configuration of the library's proxy server that changes that proxy server's URL can result in having to change all URLs in the OPAC.

As handy as proxy servers are for providing flexible solutions to remote access, they add a layer of complexity to transactions between library users and online resources. The use of federated search applications, link resolvers and the array of online tools that make up our distributed information environment only add to this complexity. If a library user is searching several OCLC and Ebsco databases from the Muse global federated search interface, the federated search server, OCLC servers and the Ebsco servers must all be working correctly for the transaction to work successfully. If the user is searching from their home then a proxy server is likely involved in the transaction. The proxy server generally checks patron authentication against some other server. It will check a student ID system server, or the library patron records on a library ILS server. In such a situation, at least five different servers must all be working correctly for an off-campus searcher to complete a basic search successfully. As we all know, network infrastructure can and does fail, as often as not at the peak of essay writing period on university campuses or any time that an instructional librarian is attempting to demonstrate research databases to a large class of students. Creating links between our different online systems and many electronic resources is a central part of our integration efforts. The point remains that we are building ever more complex systems that integrate multiple online systems. However, the likelihood and frequency of failures increases as we do so.

5.5 Getting more from link resolvers

The sharing of information between many different online systems, including link resolvers, ILS and ERM systems, vendor content and management systems, is becoming widespread. A new model of an open and interoperable information environment is taking shape, where metadata collection and maintenance is a shared responsibility and necessary information is exchanged automatically from one system to another as needed. Both libraries and systems vendors are beginning to understand the possibilities of this new model. We are starting to initiate a set of tools to develop this interoperable environment. However, at every turn we run into disconnects between the features we need, current capabilities. However, we can see that barriers of open exchange of information can be easily overcome given the modest improvements to the tools that are already available. We should expect the functionality of the suite of online tools that we are coming to rely on to get much better.

Link resolvers are a case in point. Link resolvers have provided large advances in library services in the last few years. They have been important in showing the possibilities for shared and distributed information management. Nevertheless, link resolver technology is only a few years old. Link resolvers are still a considerable way from being the integration tools we would like them to be. There are many added features and improvements to functionality that are needed before link resolvers meet the promise we can clearly see for them.

Jeff Carter's comments

A little while ago, a colleague of mine at the University of New Brunswick (UNB), Canada, wrote the following comments on the serials information shortcomings of the link resolver used in our region. Some of these shortcomings are particular to one link resolver. There is an ongoing process to provide new features. However, Jeff very insightfully outlines his institution's desire to use the link resolver to integrate all information collected about serials, to simplify the process of serials information collecting, and reduce the number of tools being used (Carter, 2007).

> At UNB we maintain a separate (locally developed and customized) e-journals database system that is still considered our de facto list for what our journal coverage/access should be. It has been running for 5 years now (it was started before we began including electronic journals in our catalogue). This list uses a partial MARC record including full library catalogue subject listings, variant titles, preceding and continued titles (all searchable) and very extensive coverage statements just as you would find in the catalogue (includes all holes in coverage, missing issues, starts and stops, etc.).

We are keen to move away from this list, to use the link resolver as primary source for serials information. However, we have invested extensive work to date and the link resolve's inability to easily duplicate that work has prevented us from doing so.

Why?

1. We have a hell of a lot of journals and journal packages (one of the largest collections in the region), so maintaining information on them all manually entirely defeats the purpose of having centrally managed collections. (Set-and-forget collections that are updated centrally in the link resolver). The resolver was supposed to make life easier for managing our serials collections, but still the answer everyone keeps coming back to for meeting all our serials information needs is to maintaining customized local holdings. This may work fine for smaller institutions. Some of them I know of are paying Serials Solutions for serials MARC records and still have to move those around and customize them.

2. We are not jumping ship, and moving away from our locally-developed serials list, only to do all the same work in a different venue, especially when we have also invested a lot of work in extensive notes and titles that cannot be applied to the managed collections. They would all have to be imported AGAIN into local holdings. The resolver collections run on their own with minimal intervention now.

3. You cannot apply custom coverage to the centrally maintained collections. Other link resolvers do have

the ability to overlay custom coverage on to the centrally managed collections. In other words, if your coverage does not match the default collection dates, you simply set custom dates for them all or individually. This overrides the defaults BUT and this is the important piece, the collection is still centrally managed and updated so you never have to worry that your title lists do not match. We keep our ScienceDirect lists in local holdings now ONLY because our current link resolver is not capable of this yet and our coverage is significantly unbalanced when it comes to comparison with the defaults.

4. Multiple start and stop dates and holes in coverage can only be represented in notes...local holdings in notes AND worse still, you cannot set single records to represent these holes. The only way is to enter the same journal record multiple times, each with a different date range in local holdings. You may say "well it is good enough", but our experience here is the more things work and work better the more people come to expect precision. If there is no easy way to record these black holes and answer patron questions about why they cannot get that particular article, there should be. I certainly think the electronic era is beyond the precision paranoia of the catalogue record but certain things like this should not mean we have to throw out an entire collection and have to keep it in local holdings. The resolvers should be less work, not more; and for us, not the same work all over again.

5. My wish list for our resolver is as follows:

1. Add the ability to have custom fields (notes, variant titles, preceding and succeeding, access notes, whatever), which do not get overwritten to all managed title lists.

2. Specifically, add the ability to add custom coverage to any record and have that be the coverage the resolver uses instead of the default vendor provided statement. Vendors are notoriously wrong, out-of-date, and misleading, and it is often not in their best interest to be precise.

3. Add the ability to have multiple coverage statements for titles. Admittedly, this is probably more work than the other two.

I know we had others but these would certainly compel us to terminate our own e-journals database. (Carter, unpublished)

Jeff sums up a number of points that are being widely discussed by people managing link resolvers.

A link resolver knowledgebase is simply a spreadsheet, or database if you like, listing metadata elements of information about each journal a library has access to. The link resolver software must find particular information in particular locations in this table in order to do its job. However, there is no technical barrier to libraries adding additional columns to this table so as to include other information they may wish to record about each serial. Libraries like the one described above at UNB would like to merge the metadata they wish to maintain for each listed journal with the metadata maintained by the link resolver company. This would result in a situation in which the link resolver company maintains some of the data elements for each serial, while the local library can add and maintain additional data elements about the same serial. Most link resolver products have no provisions for allowing libraries to customise knowledgebase tables to add their own information.

They typically give libraries the option of either letting the link resolver company manage a prescribed set of metadata elements or the library can take on all metadata management for that serial entry, as "custom" or "local holding". What most knowledgebases cannot do is to allow the library to manage some metadata elements, while leaving the link resolver company to manage others.

Link resolvers provide methods for libraries to add "custom" content. Customised information can be local holdings information, which the library adds about their paper serials or other materials the link resolver company does not know about, or it can include managed material, to which the library has made changes. Therefore, with most link resolvers, once a library changes a journal entry in the knowledgebase, it becomes "custom" coverage. The library is responsible in future for updating that journal entry. Knowledgebases contain many errors for various reasons, but if libraries correct these, then the corrected records become custom content that the link resolver company will not alter. It then becomes the responsibility of the local library to maintain and update these records in future. As libraries find and correct errors in the knowledgebase they create a larger and larger body of custom content that they must then find the time to maintain in the future. Carter makes an obvious call for a way for libraries to modify and correct the knowledgebase, but still leave the link resolver company responsible for future updates.

It is common for libraries like UNB, described above, to have developed a range of home built tools for listing and managing their electronic serials holdings. These may be databases or spreadsheets, as well as an array of paper files including everything from price and renewal information and licensing documentation. If link resolvers become more flexible, they can become general-purpose utilities, which allow libraries to store and manage their own information about electronic holdings alongside information essential to linking. If these tools become sufficiently flexible, they can then begin replacing other locally-developed tools, and allow libraries to consolidate and integrate the electronic content information that they store.

Carter also suggests that he finds the information provided by vendors in his knowledgebase to be too often inaccurate. This is a common complaint about link resolvers (Livingston *et al.*, 2006). Many library staff with whom I have talked report struggling with missing, out of date or incomplete information in their link resolving knowledgebases. A study at California State University showed students' limited success using the Ex Libris SFX link resolving. This study explored both library user and librarian perceptions of the success of link resolving. In general, they found that end users' highest priority interest was for "more full text" while librarians' greatest concern was for "more accurate results". Their testing also showed that 20 per cent of all requests to the link resolver resulted in either false positives or false negatives (Wakimoto *et al.*, 2006).

Ultimately, vendors of a particular package of e-journals must have accurate information about what products each library purchases from them. They should be expected to be able to supply complete and up to date information about the content and holdings they provide. With many changes to content and holdings taking place, this seems to be a difficult task for many publishers.

Changes of title are an area of particular concern for libraries. To find articles in journals quickly and easily it is very important to know when a journal has changed title. Frequent changes in title often result in searchers being unable to fine a needed journal. As e-journals change hands, and move from one publisher to another, the current publisher of a journal may not have full knowledge of what the journal may have been previously titled. Publishers often rely on libraries to maintain a complete record of any particular journal's title changes, over long periods, and that title may have passed through several publishers in its history.

Link resolvers uniformly maintain coverage information for large publishers and major aggregator packages. Their coverage of small publishers and individual e-journals varies a great deal. Some link resolvers offer extensive lists of linking information to individual e-journals. They also provide lists of free and open access materials. However, others leave these to be managed manually by each library.

At present, knowledgebases do not have a means of receiving customised information from vendors about each library. All too often, the only customisation tools they offer are features for creating custom content and local holdings lists where libraries must maintain their own title lists. Link resolvers typically list standardised sets of content for each vendor product or package. Vendors very often provide libraries with altered or amended versions of these packages. They offer wide variations of content in their packages. The exact journals to be included can be negotiated. Large consortia often have the buying power to get e-journal publishers to adjust titles and holdings to meet particular needs. They may negotiate the inclusion of additional content or local variations on standard years of coverage. There is an ongoing effort by publishers to add older archival material to electronic journal holdings. The current 5 or 10 year's-worth of journal materials are offered as a base product. Archival materials can then be added by each library as a supplemental product. A 5- or 10-year basic coverage in a database means that years of coverage change each year as a new year of material is added to the holdings span, and the oldest year is taken away. This means that library holdings records for that e-content package must be adjusted by 1 year. The complexities of each library's electronic holdings are considerable. It is a surprisingly difficult task to maintain complete and detailed information. Therefore, link resolver companies and content vendors have proven very helpful about fully managing title lists for library consortiums or customised packages of electronic content. However, others provide little customised support, and leave it to individual libraries to manually change lists of content in their link resolvers. Libraries typically spend a substantial amount of time double-checking information in link resolver knowledgebases and in other e-journal title lists they maintain.

Keeping track of changes to electronic serials in the library ILS, the link resolver and internal library record keeping systems is a major task. Most electronic content producers provide regular updates of changes to their content. Nevertheless, keeping track of hundreds of separate electronic content updates is an all but impossible task. Link resolvers collect this content change information from hundreds of e-content producers. Each journal added or removed, each journal title changed by electronic content publishers and vendors is collected. Some link resolvers are able to provide a regular list of changes to subscribing libraries. For libraries attempting to maintain serials changes in their ILS, regular lists of e-content changes are a major advantage of a link resolver. Although they collect it, some link resolver companies cannot provide this information as a report in human readable form. Changes are introduced into a master database of tens of thousands of online journals being tracked by the link resolver company. However, they lack the ability to extract titles that have changed each month for any particular library.

Many of the advances we look for in link resolvers are the features being developed for electronic resource management systems. We should be looking for simple changes such as greater flexibility in customising knowledgebases to individual library needs, and greater flexibility in sharing the management of knowledgebase records. Libraries must also be seeking more accurate and comprehensive information in knowledgebases, from both link resolver companies and content vendors. The possibilities are vast for link resolvers to provide libraries with even more flexible and powerful tools for integrating our electronic collections.

5.6 Package, not item, management

The electronic content package has become an essential unit of management for libraries. These include publishers' packages such as that offered by Wiley InterScience, or aggregator collections like the Gale Masterfile, or NetLibrary e-book collections. Packages allow libraries to deal with large groups of electronic serials and books, rather than managing individual items at the journal title, article and book title level. It is now common to purchase thousands of e-books. Prepared MARC records for e-book or e-serials collections, ready to be batch loaded into a library catalogue, are now common. As our e-journal collections have grown, it has become necessary to rely on vendors to provide title list information about the collections they are providing.

Content packages are a relatively new entity in libraries. Library management models remain directed at individual titles. However, libraries are finding it necessary to move away as much as possible from the old model of managing e-materials records individually. The management demands of electronic collections, the large volume of materials, and their frequent changes, make management of each individual e-book and serial title effectively impossible, with the staff and time resources most libraries have available. Libraries are doing a growing part of their e-materials management by working with large packages of electronic content. These are aggregated vendor e-serials databases, entire publisher collections, and large collections of e-books. We must look to publishers and other electronic package creators to provide the management information we need, including journal titles, exact volume and issue holdings included in each e-journal package, and ever-changing URL information.

Libraries still subscribe to many individual electronic publications. Many vendors still operate with the expectation that libraries will continue the time consuming and labour intensive practice of managing their materials individually rather than in packages. Management of some individual e-journals seems inevitable. We still strive to access the value of the material to our researchers first, and then determine how to manage the materials, even if they are not included in a convenient large package of electronic content. However, it is entirely unrealistic to attempt to evaluate the many thousands of electronic journals we now have available with the individual methods we once used for much smaller paper collections.

In my library, we are doing everything possible to find batch methods for managing individual electronic serials subscriptions. We are encouraging small publishers to recognise that methods of management need to change. Serials agents are having a key role to play in this change. Subscription agents provide aggregated invoicing and licensing services. They have largely ended the need for financial and administrative dealings with many hundreds of individual publishers.

Serials agents such as Ebsco, Swetts and Blackwell are developing sophisticated online management applications that track both the materials that can be purchased from these vendors and a great deal of information about accessing these materials. These management applications are an important resource for the libraries that use subscription agents. They are an incentive to use subscription agent services. These applications allow many libraries to benefit from serials title list information, online access and availability information collected centrally by the agents. The subscription agents have a relationship with serials publishers and the resources to maintain this information more easily and accurately than any single library. The efficiencies of serials agents' participation in the process are obvious. In a recent article Jue Wang outlined the role that subscription agent systems and services are coming to play (Wang, 2005).

The major serials agents' management applications also provide single aggregated user interface to the many hundreds of individually subscripted electronic journals. The serials agent then manages URL linking information and provides packaged title list information for all individual serials being offered through their interface. At my library, we look to Ebsco's Electronic Journal Service (EJS) whenever possible to provide a single interface to our electronic journals. We regularly work with our serials agent to get new electronic publications added to their online interface. We strongly encourage small electronic journal publishers to allow their content and licensing to be intermediated by serials subscription agents, and have their content accessible from subscription agent online interfaces such as EJS. This means the serials can be accessed and linked to using persistent URLs maintained and updated by the subscription agent, rather than less reliable individual URLs provided by the publisher. Individually subscribed journals included in a subscription agent's system can be searched as a group and can be accessed as a group of titles by our federated search application.

We are also regularly working with our link resolver provider to ensure that individual electronic journals we subscribe to are included as managed content whenever possible, so that the link resolver company will update holdings and URL linking information for these titles. Many link resolvers also manage lists of freely available content from the Directory of Open Access Journals (DOAJ) and other free and open access publications. It is often useful to ask link resolver companies to add additional materials to the content they manage from new small publishers rather than individual libraries maintaining local holdings information. We are also encouraging small electronic publishers to add their content to available profit and not-for-profit aggregations such as DOAJ, Ingenta and HireWire press, rather than managing their content individually. Even as libraries move to more and more packaged management of electronic content, individual electronic item subscriptions will continue to present special challenges.

The advent of large electronic collections has also changed our methods of collection development a great deal. As with other processes, our methods of collection selection are based on manual processes, and the individual selection of each item to be included in the library collections. We have been using automation for years to create profiles for the selection of books, standing orders and approval plans. Libraries have been recognising for some time that individual assessment of each item to be purchased is often not viable given the volume of material to be selected. This has become even truer with the purchase of large packages of electronic materials. It has been essential to deal with a growing volume of material with limited resources. The assessment and selecting of the individual titles most pertinent to each library collection is giving way to the more general selection of broadly relevant packages based on reviews, reputation and some sampling of available materials. This package management approach to collecting has presented some new problems. The matter of overlapping serials content available in multiple online products is one of the most obvious. If libraries are to make sound collection choices, package management requires a level of analysis that has never been necessary with individual materials selection. Libraries need to be turning more and more to automation to assist in collection evaluation. Tools like Ulrich's Serials Analysis Service are available. This is another area where link resolvers are providing libraries with important new services. Some link resolvers offer useful collection evaluation tools. Many libraries have developed their own title list analysis spreadsheets and databases. Each of these offers title list comparisons for available online content packages, analysis of the titles that overlap between different online packages and a means of sorting electronic collections by subject in order to assess their strengths in different disciplines. New automated collection assessment tools make it possible to make changes to collections much more rapidly than ever before, determine what are the most popular or subject relevant packages of materials for users and rapidly changing large volumes of content to adjust accordingly. Rather than selecting individual content titles, electronic collections development is increasingly about cost benefit analysis; simply ensuring that the relevant and newly available content we are adding to our collections is worth the cost, despite inevitable duplication of content between different packages. As our collections of electronic materials get larger, the amount of both subject and title duplication becomes greater.

Electronic product offering are also becoming much more diverse. In addition to electronic serials and electronic book collections there are also a growing number of packages from publishers such as Alexander Street Press, Gale or Chadwick Healy that are mixtures of content. They include primary and secondary sources, journal articles and selections from books, and as well as new and unique editorial content. They are more like the selected and edited content of textbooks or reference works than the full-text serials databases that libraries have come to know in recent years. Many such products blur the line between journal collections, reference materials and e-books. Libraries must rely largely on the reputation of the publisher as regards to the quality, completeness and balance of the selected content. As the range of available online materials continues to grow, detailed and in depth methods of assessing packages of online materials for overlap, subject coverage, and quality will only become more essential.

5.7 Staffing, skills, vendor hosting and distributed management

The management of library materials used to be handled by a small number of library staff centred on cataloguing activities in ILSs. A wider group of library staff are now involved with the management of electronic collections; they require a broad new range of skills. Different departments in libraries often manage the disparate but closely linked group of electronic materials systems. In my library, the Acquisitions Department oversees access to the serials agent's database, which provides lists of serials titles with individual online licences, as well as spreadsheets and other tools for managing the purchase of online materials. Cataloguing departments have a different workflow for maintenance of library catalogue records for the electronic materials, which we catalogue. The Cataloguing Department maintains URLS in MARC 856 fields. Cataloguers track changes to the content in full-text serials databases so that changes to the library catalogue can be made. Our Systems Department handles administration of the many individual serials database interfaces. The Systems Department also handles management of the link resolver, federated search application and administration of individual e-content databases. Our User Instruction librarians handle management of the Citation Management application. Another department and several interlocking document delivery consortia manage the library's nationwide Document Delivery system. As my library participates in one consortium for federated search and link resolving, staff work collectively to make decisions about the development of these shared tools. We also participate in a different consortium for our ILS. There is also a congenial and collegiate process for decision making in this regard. These cooperative efforts work remarkably well, and I am fortunate to work with a group of very professional colleagues. Again, there is nothing remarkable about the arrangements in my library and our regional consortia. The details are different for each library, but these inter-departmental and inter-consortia complexities are becoming the norm.

Libraries are building far-reaching and flexible highly distributed management systems. These distributed systems are not unlike webpage content management systems such as Macro Media Contribute. The people most directly involved with particular information maintain that information on the larger system. Many employees input information into the system, and utilise information from its different components. The contributors to the system include individual library staff, staff working for one or more library consortium, staff of different software vendors, as well as serials agents, book dealers and many different publishers and content vendors. These emerging distributed reintegrated systems are made up of link resolving, federated search, and the other systems that I have described, in addition to the ILS.

Libraries, service, and content vendors have been slow to fully or formally recognise these component systems as parts in a larger structure. The linking and exchange of information between systems is sometimes ad hoc and customised in many cases. However, the shape of the new modular interoperable component system that we are building is well established.

One of the most common complaints that I hear about library staffing is that staff lack the skills needed to implement service improvements and better integration between their systems. Much work tying different systems together requires specialised technological skills and custom programming skills. Too many of the components of the emerging distributed management structure are not yet available off the shelf. Improvements to library systems and better systems integration are still dependent on a host of customisations to individual library systems. As long as service improvements are dependent on PHP, PERL or SQL and Oracle skills, libraries will struggle in their integration efforts. Larger libraries, which can bring skilled people to their projects, must lead the way.

The skills shortage is one of the increasing number of barriers to libraries moving forward successfully with automated and distributed materials management and their emerging information integration role. Many library systems, ILSs among them, are seen as complex and arcane, particularly by library staff that come to managing them with relatively little background and training. The developers of these systems will maintain that this is the nature of the complex, highly configurable work that libraries are undertaking.

To some extent, the growing reliance on high-level systems skills is unavoidable. Yet, there are a growing number of examples of powerful and complex systems that are simple to operate and administer. Online journal aggregators offer complex interfaces that search many millions of items. They offer online administrative interfaces that library staff can be taught to use in a few hours.

A growing number of the systems that libraries rely on are vendor hosted. System vendors take on the complexities of managing servers and software. They simply provide libraries with online applications such as federated search software, link resolver and citation management systems that can be managed by local libraries using simple web-based administrative tools.

Only a couple of years ago, most libraries and certainly large academic libraries would have dismissed the idea of housing critical information resources for any individual library on a vendor's remote website, and relying on the connections via the Internet for access. Until recently, Internet connectivity was still too unreliable and our trust in vendors was too limited. However, today many libraries make arrangements for vendors to even host their ILSs. As the use of full text developed, our users quickly became dependent on vendor-hosted databases such as Ebsco Academic or Gale Infotrac. Almost before we realised it, the popularity of these resources made them every bit as essential a resource as the library catalogue.

Hosted services are an essential part of the new more efficient, automated and integrated materials management model that libraries are building. Most of the new electronic materials systems are already hosted by vendors rather than being maintained by libraries. The bulk of e-journal and e-book databases are entirely hosted by vendors. Link resolving and federated search applications seem to be a mixed environment with larger libraries and early adapting libraries tending to have locally managed software running on their own servers. The largest libraries will likely continue to prefer to host their own applications, and there are advantages to doing so because the individual library system has greater control and flexibility in hosting its own systems. Larger libraries are also the most likely to have sufficient trained technical staff to manage locally-hosted systems. In addition, they have the expertise to customise applications and get the most out of the flexibility of locally-hosted systems.

Local hosted servers are still important in some library applications, where the server operating system, database software and application system software must all be managed individually. It is common for ILSs, web servers, proxy servers and institutional deposit systems to each have their own locally-hosted server operating system and software. Libraries still rely heavily on UNIX and Linux and Windows operating system skills and associated programming and database management skills. Currently, staff must often apply attention and scarce resources to the technical management of their systems. However, the movement to vendor-hosted applications is gaining momentum.

Overall, the vendor-hosted systems benefit from economies of scale. They require much less expertise on the part of library staff. Centralised, vendor-hosted services benefit from ongoing feature enhancement, as vendors improve and update central service sites. It is common for libraries to purchase an application such as a federated search tool, or an ILS, and then not have enough funding or the expertise to update it as they would like to have.

Through vendor hosting libraries have an opportunity to seek simplified administrative and materials management products to reduce their reliance on specialised technological skills. It is common for locally-hosted ILSs to remain little changed for years once a library has gone through the arduous task of implementing a new system. In the new environment, vendors of hosted systems are making hundreds of changes each year, without the need for customisation by each library, or involvement by specialised library systems staff. The model of locally-hosted ILS change is out of step with what is happening with hosted applications elsewhere in the online information environment.

The process of lowering the skills threshold applies as much to our to patron services as it does to our administrative processes. It is still too common to see library online services where users are presented with one or several pages of instructions for use. "If you use Internet Explorer follow these instructions", "If you use Firefox click here". It is also common to see libraries, proud of new services they are introducing, present users with lengthy introductory information, explaining the new service project, the organisations involved, project funding, and the great benefits of the new service. Then users are presented with instructions for using the new service. Library users seem to have a diminishing tolerance of any large amounts of introductory text or lengthy instructions.

In my experience, we have often found ourselves seeking ways of overcoming library users' reluctance to receive the instruction needed to develop new skills. We often encounter the same difficulty introducing library staff to new and complex management processes. We have seen many library services, from search interfaces to online document delivery forms, simplified greatly in the last few years. We have often discovered that the problem is not how to get those who use a process to absorb the necessary training; the problem is usually how to improve, streamline and simplify a system, so that less training is necessary. I have often found that if a new online library service requires more than a few lines of instruction for users to understand its operation, more instructional information is not the answer. Most often, the service's processes are too complex and need to be rethought. The most successful user interfaces operate on the assumption that no instruction is needed. This is certainly the case with major Internet sites and search engines.

Our role should be to continuously look for ways to simplify the systems that we use and lower the skills required of our library users and staff, as we strive to make each service simple enough to be used directly without intermediaries. Embracing disintermediation is not easy for library services that see themselves first as intermediaries. It means that our role with some services will be to work ourselves out of a job, as we are able to disintermediate these services. Libraries can do this with the expectation that there are many opportunities to successfully apply our skills in new service areas.

5.8 Costs of new systems, rich and poor libraries and the new digital divide

The many components of the new distributed electronic information environment all come with substantial costs. Electronic content products take up a growing portion of library budgets. Many libraries are strictly limited in the online resources they can afford. Integration tools such as link resolving, federated search applications and ERM systems are becoming essential to the modern library's role. Yet there are a great many libraries that cannot afford the increasing costs of the fast-developing tools. ILS and other system vendors are developing new and innovative services. These include enhanced searching, sophisticated resource discovery tools, as well as flexible and detailed statistical reporting applications and improved electronic resource management features. Too many of these innovations are not being added as enhancements or new core features to existing ILSs. Instead, innovative services are only available as value added, additional cost, extended features, or as entirely new applications that work side by side with existing library systems.

At the same time, the pace of ILS change has traditionally been slow. Libraries have replaced their ILSs infrequently. ILS vendors, selling only a small number of systems have been revamping their product lines at a modest pace. In the fast-developing information environment, libraries require much more rapid innovation, enhancement and modification to their systems. In many cases, libraries have customised their own solutions. In other cases, new, more nimble applications have grown up to meet service needs. Libraries are now confronting a new digital divide, between libraries that can afford the online content resources and distributed applications of the new information environment, and those that cannot afford enhanced applications. The divide separates libraries that can deploy federated search, link resolving and advanced search interfaces such as Endeca, Primo or Aqua-browser, from libraries that can offer only a more limited OPAC and selected individual online resources. It divides libraries that can apply skilled staff time to customising innovative integrated services from libraries that can only deploy basic vendor supplied services.

Other new advancements to library services also divide libraries that can pay from those that cannot pay. These include vendor supplied MARC records, URL information and enhanced content such as cover images. Libraries obtain a great deal of their MARC data free of charge today. Copy cataloguing is widespread. A growing number of publishers and publishing agents also provide digital MARC data, if not free, at least as a built-in cost of publication. In the e-book market, publishers are struggling to expand sales. They also recognise that the purchase of large groups of e-books presents a problem for over-stretched library cataloguing operations. Thus, it is common for batch MARC data to be included in the purchase of e-books. Libraries need to work as a group to encourage the trend toward making batch MARC information available at the lowest possible cost. Yet libraries still spend a great deal of money purchasing MARC information. Many library catalogues lack supplemental information and 856 field links because of a shortage of funds to purchase enhanced cataloguing.

Libraries need to be working together and with publishers to make these resources widely and uniformly available rather having only the most well funded of libraries able to afford them. Luckily, innovation, imagination and hard work on the part of library staff can offset shortages of funding. Good use of open source software and freely available resources can still provide scope for developing innovative library services. Thus, our efforts at creating an integrated information environment must focus on providing uniform services available to all libraries.

5.9 Information preservation

The preservation role of libraries is another area where there is major change in the new environment of electronic library materials. As libraries have greatly increased the amount of leased electronic materials in their collections, they have deemphasised their role in maintaining materials in perpetuity. To some extent this is inevitable. It is not reasonable for libraries to pay the same attention to the preservation of large electronic collections of leased materials that they once applied to our smaller paper collections.

Several decades ago my library maintained a collection of several thousand journals titles. Once purchased, these materials were expected to remain in our collection indefinitely. We saw it as our role to maintain a permanent collection of these materials. Today, the same library stewards collections of electronic and paper journals that are five times larger. Our coverage of these journals is influenced by many embargoes, which are between 1 and 5 years in length. Many of our database subscriptions provide a rolling period of current coverage. As an example, only the current 10 year's-worth of material might be available. This means that each year, 1 year's worth of material ceases to be available to our users.

It is a common occurrence for journal coverage to end in a database, because that journal has moved to another publisher or arrangement for offering online access to that journal have changed. In our relatively modest collection, hundreds of journal titles change each year. This relative collection instability is a price we have willingly paid for the fivefold increase in the overall number journals we can make available, and widespread online user access to that material. It is a bargain well worth making, until you are the researcher who has been working with 10-year-old journal materials only to wake up on January 1st of a new year to discover that database coverage has moved on, and your journal materials are no longer available. With much larger collections, libraries are often hard pressed to even be aware when important journal titles are removed from a database. When this does happen, libraries have a broader range of alternative access options than ever before. Many libraries have focused their attention on providing users with the largest possible pool of current and relatively recent materials, rather than on long-term preservation. This is particularly true with smaller libraries, which are increasingly leaving the issue of preservation to larger libraries, if they give it much thought at all.

If the underlying goal of libraries is to work toward more universal access to materials, offering only shifting accumulations of recent materials does not meet this goal.

But falling back to pre-digital ways of thinking is clearly not an answer to this problem.

The long-standing preservation mission of libraries has relied on duplication and good fortune to protect published works. There has never been a comprehensive effort to ensure that publishers and major research libraries preserver bodies of materials. When Elsevier went through the process of digitising a full collection of materials, the company published back to the 1820s. They worked with several of the largest research libraries in the world, but still they found a small but significant number of Elsevier journal issues that were very difficult, or impossible to locate. The online back file will never be 100 per cent complete according the Elsevier backfile project head Lindi Belfield (Elsevier, 2002). So even with archives from one of the most prominent STM publishers in the world and access to the collections of several major research libraries, there were still materials that have been lost. Our preservation efforts under the old system were not completely successful and yet they were the best methods possible given the available resources and technology.

Budget pressures and movement to electronic collections are in some ways doing libraries a favour by forcing them to move away from the notion of permanently retaining everything. As we have adapted to a more fluid model of electronic collections management, we are becoming more aware of how rapidly books and serials become dated, and their limited useful shelf life for most users. Only a small percentage of our collections are currently relevant to the great majority of our users. Most library users would happily trade long-term preservation of materials for a bigger collection of current and easily accessible materials. We often lament that fact that libraries are seen as static collections of dusty old books. If our role is to provide the greatest amount of material to meet immediate users' needs, then emphasising currently available electronic materials and deemphasising preservation is a sound strategy. With limited time and resources, the average college or public library is focusing on putting the greatest amount of currently relevant material in to the hands of the most users. Ready online access to global library catalogues, better document delivery services, major digitisation efforts such as Google Books, improving online coverage of journal materials – these all make it easier than ever to locate and access virtually any published work. This enables many libraries to move away from notions of preservation and focus on providing what is immediately relevant.

Libraries have been taking a less active role in preservation for some time. The presence of fully digitised collections will continue to lessen individual libraries attention to preservation. If we know that all Springer or Oxford or Wiley journals are available online, obviously we will not feel so great an obligation to maintain our paper collections of obscure runs of journals from one of these publishers. It has become common practice for libraries to discontinue subscribing to journals in paper because copies are available in electronic form. In the past we might have checked union catalogues before deciding to discard a particular journal. It has not been unusual to discover that we are the only library in the country or the region to hold a particular run of journals. In the digital environment this preservation concern is much less likely to play a part in our decision making. It is easy to argue the folly of libraries deemphasising their preservation role. The focus only on current and most popular materials may well cause problems in the long run, but it is nonetheless a reality in many smaller libraries.

Of course libraries collectively continue to have an

important obligation to preservation of published materials and collections. This role has always fallen disproportionately on larger research libraries. The effort to digitise materials represents an enormous effort and achievement on behalf of the many agencies involved. This digitisation effort should provide a better preservation situation than has ever existed before. Complete works will be available and fully documented in a way that was never before possible. However, digital storage formats and storage media are volatile, prone to change and degradation. It will be a very substantial task to preserve the vast digital collections that are being created. A commitment to preserving the complete body of worldwide library holdings is probably more important than ever before. The current movement away from addressing preservation concerns by many libraries is a matter of circumstance, though it is undoubtedly short sighted. There are a number of efforts underway to address preservation issues including LOCKSS and related initiatives (LOCKSS, 2007). Therefore, both large and small libraries need to find collective ways of meeting the growing challenges of preservation

6

Whither the OPAC: new models for the primary library search interface

In the new distributed information environment in which libraries are participating and helping to develop, there are many content access issues. The library's primary public interface, the OPAC, is just one access tool, which provides limited access to a small part of the online information environment. Libraries are rethinking the OPAC in light of changes in the environment and the new search tools available to our users.

There has been broad agreement for some time that the access capabilities of OPAC systems are limited; Roy Tennant and Andrew Pace famously used the term "lipstick on a pig" to describe superficial or essentially cosmetic efforts over the last few years to improve the search capabilities of today's OPACs. As Roy Tennant commented:

> I am not the only one frustrated with the current state of our integrated library systems (ILS). North Carolina State University's Andrew Pace (from whom I first heard the "lipstick on a pig" reference) and others have been bemoaning the sad state of systems. We should listen.

Oh, you can blame library vendors for not tackling this problem, but there is plenty of blame to go around. The library market has become a battle of attrition, where new customers are found by stealing them. In this zero-sum game, vendors partly rely on how painful it is to change systems and that it takes an egregious situation to force a library to jump ship.

Meanwhile, we are focused on making our own lives easier rather than the lives of our patrons. The user-focused enhancements that do make it through generally reflect incremental changes rather than deep, systemic improvements that will create the systems our users need. For that kind of leadership and courage, only the vendor can devote the required resources.

Think big

Libraries with sufficient resources should experiment with other methods of making their collections searchable. High-profile experiments in bibliographic database search systems may help point the way for vendors not eager to perform major redesign projects. A prime example is the Research Library Group's RedLightGreen, a beacon of hope in a sea of library catalogue disasters. OCLC is also pushing the envelope, as a recent blog posting by Lorcan Dempsey, the OCLC Vice President, illustrates.

So what can most of us do? We need to focus more energy on important, systemic changes rather than cosmetic ones. If your system is more difficult to search and less effective than Amazon.com (and whose is not?), then you have work to do. Stop asking for minor tweaks from vendors. After all, you can put lipstick on a pig, but it is still very much a pig. (Tennant, 2005)

Since Roy Tennant issued this call for changes to library OPACs, there has been a focus on improving the functionality of the library primary search tool. Providing tools that more fully realise users' search needs and expectations, and begin to match the powerful search services provided by other online search tools is essential. In a recent article, Andrew Pace notes the importance of "next generation library catalogue search tools".

Next-gen acronyms

For decades, the ILS has been the primary computerized management tool for libraries. For inventory control, it still works pretty darn well. On the resource-discovery front, talk of "next generation catalogs" has led to several discussions of what exactly a catalog should be, as well as new and exciting vendor developments like ExLibris' Primo, Innovative Interface's Encore, and rapidly increasing sales of Medialab's AquaBrowser. Encore and Primo will be attractive newcomers to this sphere. Local and open source development also continues – the Florida Center for Library Automation and Phoenix Public Library have launched their own Endeca-powered catalog interfaces, and IndexData displayed an impressive metasearch engine with faceted navigation at Midwinter. (Pace, 2007)

Search methods that group results by subject, or determine the subject relevancy of results are making more complete use of the subject headings and other cataloguing metadata that libraries have recorded in the catalogue but have often made relatively little use of. The ability to quickly divide search results by subject is an example. A searcher might wish to view materials that contain the word "tree", but only those works in the subject area of computer science regarding tree structures in programming, not biology or botany works related to trees, or any other form of tree structure. A modern search interface should be able to divide the search results by subject, rapidly allowing the searcher to focus thus on the material most relevant to their needs. Such enhanced search features have been needed in library catalogues for some time. Similar features are commonplace for many search resources on the web. The search services are setting the bar for library OPACs are often the large e-content aggregators. Companies such as Ebsco, CSA/Proquest and Gale are driven by strong competition. They have been at the forefront in providing new and innovative search tools. They rapidly deploy new interface features in a way not possible with ILSs. New features immediately become part of the core features of their interface products. Library users have every right to expect the search services they see in EbscoHost or Proquest Illumina to be available in their library catalogues.

Applications such as Endeca, Aquabrowser and Ex Libris Primo are a major step forward for the OPAC. They provide users with innovative search and access features, and make better use of the rich information resource of the library catalogue. The University of North Carolina was one of the first libraries to pioneer the advanced features of Endeca search software (Antelman *et al.*, 2006). Yet this implementation required regular extraction of the bibliographic data from the ILS, then insertion and re-indexing in another database system. In the same way, Ross Singer at Georgia TechFirstly has described extracting and re-indexing the data from his ILS and re-indexing using the open source indexing engine Zebra (Singer, 2006). The fact that was necessary is a telling comment on the inflexibility of ILSs.

Restricted database licences are one of the barriers to

innovative use of ILSs. Licences often prevent libraries from storing additional data, creating additional indexes, or otherwise using ILS databases in innovative ways. Even when licensing does not prevent it, ILSs are often too complex to be easily or safely adapted to interact with other systems at the SQL relational database level. Libraries should be looking for ways to have search interface innovations quickly and universally available without endless incremental costs for new vendor systems.

OCLC's Vice President, Lorcan Dempsey, also commented that "There has been a recent emphasis on the creation of an external catalogue discovery system, which takes ILS data and makes it work harder in a richer user interface"(Dempsey, 2006). From the perspective of managing electronic-collections, enhanced searching will demand both timelier and more accurate metadata. Consistent use of subject headings and their adoption over time, consistent use of names, the inclusion of more table of content information, as well as accurate and up to date e-serials information, all become much more important with better search interfaces that expose this metadata, and clearly expose the absence or inaccuracy of metadata.

6.1 Distributed search and materials management

The basic notion that libraries must store all information about their "collections" in a single monolithic database, maintained by each individual library, is out of date. It is a notion that causes a great deal of duplication of effort. It has led libraries to add quantities of electronic material to their collections that will ultimately be unsupportable. The notion that libraries should focus their users' search efforts on a single database accessing only their local collection is equally outdated, and diminishes the range of search services libraries can offer their users. Improving the search capabilities of today's OPAC systems is an important undertaking. However, libraries need to go further than providing better search capabilities for their existing OPACs. They need to fundamentally challenge the underlying concept of the centralised library catalogue.

The ability to search more than one database at a time has been a common feature available to libraries since the wide deployment of the Z39.50 search standard. However, the development of federated search software is presenting a host of new options and possibilities for distributed searching of groups of databases. The coming of link resolvers means that all metadata related to library materials access does not need to be stored in the single silo that is the library ILS. Needed metadata and the materials it describes can be linked to across the network. It is entirely possible to store some information in the ILS, while storing other information exclusively in a link resolver knowledgebase, as an example. The two can then be simultaneously searched, with a federated search tool or a Z39.50 search interface. The results can then be merged and presented to the user as a single result set.

Once it becomes common to store cataloguing information in several different systems and to share the responsibility for maintaining metadata, we begin to see the library OPAC search interface quite differently. It seems essential for libraries to start seeing their primary search tool as the central discovery and access tool for a collection of distributed resources, and not merely as the interface to one single database. Distributed searching of many independent resources is fundamental to today's World Wide Web. Fast and efficient indexing of distributed resources is basic to the Internet. The benefits of distributed searching of multiple databases have been clear to libraries for many years.

Experiments with distributed union catalogues are longstanding. It is becoming apparent that the OPAC of the future should no longer simply allow users to search whatever can be put into the library catalogue. Libraries now have the ability to decide what groups of distributed resources should be offered to users in different circumstances. They have the ability to offer one OPAC-like primary library interface or a wide selection of interfaces for use by different users in different situations.

As document delivery and consortium sharing arrangements become more extensive, there are more and more reasons to make multiple resource searches the standard search. It seems likely that library users will continue to be interested primarily in seeing a listing of everything that is readily available to them. This can include materials that can be delivered from other nearby libraries and might include materials that can be ordered at reasonable cost and delivered quickly.

From a management point of view, we can easily make materials from the Ingenta document delivery system available to our users, but practically we would not attempt to add all Ingenta-accessible journal titles to our ILSs. We know we cannot practically merge our library collections with other consortium partner libraries. If we are to provide library users with seamless access to all the research material we can provide, then the Online Public Access Catalogue must become the unifying interface to a wide array of separate online resources. My own library is a case in point. It is a little ridiculous to for us to concern ourselves only with the local holdings of our library when discussing the materials we can offer our users. Putting the World Wide Web and inter-library lending aside, and considering only the materials we actively steward, our users have immediate access to the following materials:

- Books, journals and periodicals held in our building, or in off site storage.
- Materials available for loan from our province wide consortium partners, with a 3-day delivery.
- Course specific e-materials available from Web CT and several related course management systems.
- Materials available from our regional consortium partner libraries in three adjoining provinces, with a 3-day delivery.
- e-Journal materials available in full text under licence from hundreds of publishers and suppliers.
- e-Book materials available from dozens of publishers and suppliers.
- e-Serials materials available at low cost from the national science library, with 2- or 3-day delivery.

In all, materials we can readily provide to users come from 19 Colleges and Universities, hundreds of publishers and vendors, and one national library. These materials come in dozens of formats, both paper and electronic. I am always happy to give credit to the excellent work done by my local consortium, Novanet, in Nova Scotia, Canada and the Council of Atlantic University Libraries (CAUL), in addition to the Canadian Institute of Science and Technology (CISTI). Nevertheless, the point is that ours is the normal library experience today, and not especially noteworthy.

Many library consortia would lengthen this list

considerably. What is more noteworthy is that we still consider our consortium OPAC to be the primary search interface for our users although it searches only a fraction of the materials listed above. We have developed a federated search application that searches the sources available to our users (Figure 6.1). I have to confess that my library users cannot yet search all of these materials in a single seamless search, leading them to access or obtain wanted material directly. However, that single search is what we are aiming for.

There is a clear opportunity to turn library OPACs into more expansive and comprehensive search interfaces that search a wide selection of materials that are readily

Figure 6.1   Increasingly complex distributed library search

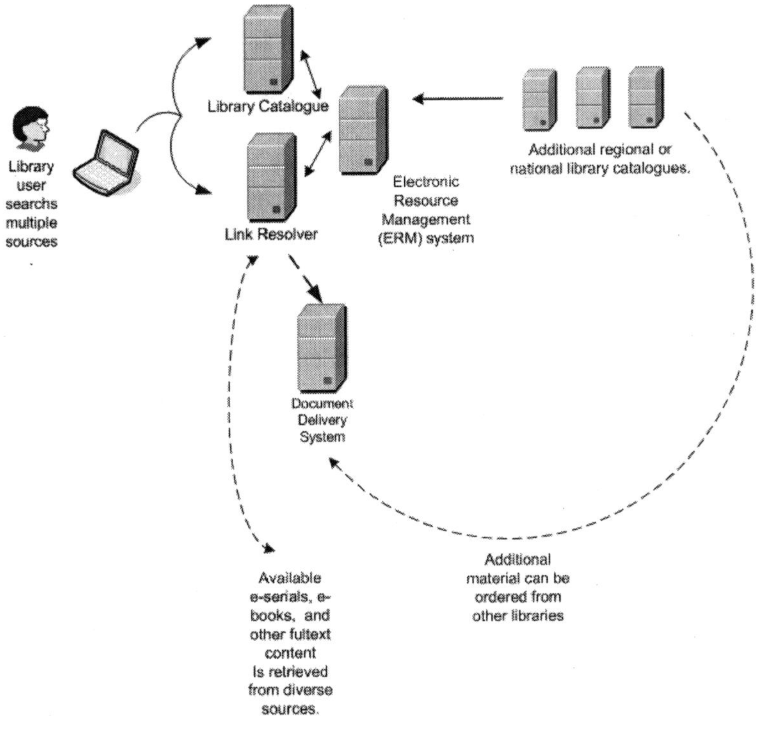

Library user searchs multiple sources

Library Catalogue

Additional regional or national library catalogues.

Electronic Resource Management (ERM) system

Link Resolver

Document Delivery System

Available e-serials, e-books, and other fultext content is retrieved from diverse sources.

Additional material can be ordered from other libraries

available to a library's users. Current ILS search tools and federated search applications clearly demonstrate the capability to do this. These search tools also have the potential to take us beyond "one size fits all" single primary library interfaces. Libraries are beginning to have the tools at their disposal to offer dozens of different search interfaces that provide appropriate materials to different users in various situations.

Unfortunately, in practice a number of barriers remain to fully realising the distributed search tools that we need. I find it difficult to understand why federated search applications and ILSs are still seen as entirely separate systems. So far, there is very little overlap in services between the two. Even enhanced search tools such as Endeca and Primo are focused primarily on improving the search capabilities of a single ILS repository, not on extending OPAC search capabilities to multiple repositories.

ILS search interfaces typically have made little progress in providing access via federated search exchange protocols. A growing number of ILSs provide services for OAI harvesting, but they generally cannot search using the SRW\SRU standard search protocol for full-text databases or the various XML-based interchange protocols being used in federated searching. They have very little capability to search repositories other than Z39.50-based library catalogues. Some have limited customisable tools for exchanging searches with other systems. They do not easily support the ability to broadcast search. Library systems have focused largely on Z39.50 standard searching, and made little effort to develop XML or other sorts of search capability to access multiple databases. My library's ILS has no built-in methods of searching non-Z39.50 compliant link resolvers. This makes it difficult to store serials records exclusively in the link resolver and then search the two systems together to display common results to the user.

Many link resolving applications do not have a Z39.50 search interface, so library catalogue search tools cannot easily search them. This is understandable as link resolvers are not typically MARC formatted databases. However, the ability to search both a journals A-to-Z list provided by a link resolver and the library catalogue simultaneously in a single search is an obvious feature sought by many libraries.

The federated search application in use in my regional library consortium is a very powerful and highly configurable industry-leading product. We have built a number of search interfaces with it. It can be used to search both our consortium library catalogue and a collection of the library catalogues of libraries with which we have borrowing agreements. Nevertheless, federated search applications have no means of providing much important OPAC functionality, so they cannot begin to replace any single individual library OPAC.

There is a great deal of user functionality in the OPAC in addition to search functionality. Users order books to be delivered from one library to another; they place holds on books others have checked out; they view what they have checked out and what fines they have, if any. However, federated search applications have no capability to offer any library catalogue functions other than search. They do not provide support for the non-bibliographic features of ILSs. NCIP searching is not supported, so it is not possible to integrate the patron authentication features and services of library OPAC into federated search applications. A user might search multiple library catalogues along with several other databases using a federated search application but they cannot look up which books they have checked out or renew a book or pay any fines owing. For these functions, they must return to our native OPAC. As libraries routinely use federated search software to search library catalogues as well as other databases, libraries should be seeking all the featured needed to replace the OPAC interface, or at least fully duplicate these interfaces with more expansive and flexible federated search interfaces.

Several federated search applications that I have encountered also do not have search targets available for directly searching link resolvers. The federated search interface provides links from search results to the link resolver to locate full text. But it is not possible to do a simultaneous database search of the link resolver along with several other databases. So again, the ability to do one federated search of several library catalogues and a serials list provided by the link resolver is not readily available. Integrating ILSs, link resolvers and federated search tools is more difficult than it should be. As we work with library users searching for information on these systems on a daily basis, we must believe that a good distributed search environment where all of these excellent tools work seamlessly together is just around the corner. The missing interface tools needed to tie these systems together are not difficult to develop. It is usually possible to overcome some of the integration barriers between these different systems by custom programming the various interfaces.

6.2 Distributed/federated search problems still to be overcome

The federated or distributed searching methods we have developed to date have been very valuable and successful.

However, as with link resolvers, there is still much to improve and many basic issues to be addressed.

For many years, we have accepted the idea of searching journal articles separately from books and journal volumes. We have carried that decision into the development of e-journal databases and article abstracting tools that search electronic serials content separate from books and journal volumes searched in the library catalogue. Federated searching does not begin to resolve the issues regarding searching different types of materials.

The search capabilities of federated search software remain quite limited compared to searching with any major native specialised search interface, including OPACs. Even federated search companies acknowledge that federated searching is a useful addition to individual search interfaces. Libraries have long accepted that we cannot begin to duplicate the article indexing efforts of the journal databases we use. Sociofile, MLA, Psychlit, etc., were created because libraries individually do not have the resources to index the discipline specific literature. One of the expectations we must have for federated searching is that it will reduce the number of individual search interfaces. To do this, federated search applications must be able to search multiple databases well enough so that users no longer have a need to use many individual interfaces. If federated searching becomes truly effective, then the searching of individual native interfaces will decline. Electronic publishers will in many cases provide content; users will not need to use their separate interface for searching. As the search capabilities of federated search applications become more complete, library ILSs can also become repositories of catalogue information that rely on one or several common federated search interfaces to search these together with other repositories of metadata.

The current methods of federated searching involve the on-going work by software companies to make fundamentally incompatible database systems compatible. A great deal of translation and integration must go on in the background for federated searching to function. This ongoing work must take place as each search target database changes how it operates. A common search can only be performed on databases that share common indexing. There is no point performing a federated search of several databases for materials indexed with a particular library of congress subject heading if the databases being searched do not maintain indexes of library congress subject terms. Federated search applications use a selection of different methods to pass searches to many databases and receive results back.

There has also been a lot of ongoing work to make the tools for passing searches to databases better. Many electronic resources are taking federated searching seriously into account and thus, working with federated search companies to develop sophisticated and standardised means, such as NISO's new MXG standard, for passing searches search results in and out of their systems. Too many online content resources still make little provision for being searched by federated search interfaces. For these, federated search companies still must resort to whatever methods they can devise, including screen scraping. This is the primitive business of taking the output from an online system, intended for end user screen display, and using it as a means of connecting that system to some other online system. It relies on the fact that web-based systems must present information to their users and receive instructions from users by passing information over the web. Methods of this kind are obviously less reliable and less functional than having direct access to database indexes. The quality of federated search results varies a great deal from online resource to online resource, as does the link resolver support, citation software support and many other services offered by individual content databases. The cost of providing wide-ranging federated search interconnections is high. Federated search companies vary in the time, resources and skills they have to put into keeping connections functioning effectively. The considerable costs and shortcomings of this imperfect process are passed on to libraries.

There is a practical limit to the number of simultaneous searches that can be performed at one time. Internet capabilities have grown, but each search still takes time to perform and return results. If results are all to be received and sorted into a single result set, then the user must wait until all results are received, before a sort can be done. In a world where convenience is paramount, searchers typically concentrate on the first search results they receive. Searchers who rely on the results available most quickly risk missing better search results simply because they take longer. The speed and convenience of federated searching continues to be a limitation. Broadcast searching quickly becomes unworkable when more than a dozen or so targets are searched. Broadcast federated searching offers no real solution for those interested in searching all available library resources with one single search.

Federated search as it is currently available has its limitations. It is nonetheless a critical resource for merging groups of resources and metadata repositories together to more easily manage and better integrate the resources we offer our users. I still commonly encounter online content producers who show little concern for the federated search accessibility and other integration features offered by their products. Libraries need to be routinely asking every online content supplier questions about the kind of search exchange ports they make available, and the federated search protocols that they support. Better federated search capabilities are critical to better integrating online resources and successful distributed management of electronic materials.

6.3 Divergence of e-content and e-interface

The electronic resources we use today all feature the same basic components. They feature descriptive information about materials. This includes indexing and abstracting metadata, and library cataloguing information. The electronic content itself is a separate component. Content commonly includes electronic books and full-text periodicals but also audio recordings, images and in fact any object that can be stored in digital form. Content and metadata must be stored in a database or repository. To search metadata and access content there must be a user interface. Interface software provides search services and presents search results to users. It may also link to other services or interfaces that may display full text, or offer additional options for searching. These are well-known basic components of all electronic content services. Is important to remember that these components can be offered in a wide range of combinations. Libraries have mostly been tightly restricted to set combinations of user interface, metadata and content repository. For example, each library's OPAC interface accesses the cataloguing information in its ILS database, the Ebsco Host user interface accesses full-text content and indexing metadata only for e-journal databases purchased from Ebsco, while the CSA/Proquest Illumina interface accesses only databases purchased from CSA. These pairings are increasingly getting in the way of the most effective management of electronic materials and the best user access to materials. It is entirely possible to have many search interfaces search the same collection of metadata to provide access to content. It is also possible to develop one interface that can access multiple repositories of information.

I have written previously (Webster, 2004) on the divergence of electronic search and retrieval interfaces, and electronic content itself. This divergence means that content and metadata are separate products from the search interface software that may be used to search them. Content does not necessarily have to be tied to a particular search interface, nor must a search interface be tied to particular content or metadata source.

Library ILSs have an important role to play in this divergence. Libraries are accessing information in library catalogues with a growing number of tools, ranging from advanced search interfaces, to searches imbedded in web pages, course management tools or browser toolbars, to federated search applications and centralised network resources such as Open WorldCat. ILSs do not have to interact only with a single search interface; they provide information to many different search interfaces. They can serve as a vital metadata repository that provides an appropriate set of services to meet the needs of a variety of search interfaces, input and extraction methods.

At the same time, it is increasingly clear that library users need to be able to search a variety of resources through their local library's OPAC, not just the physical holdings of their library, or the limited set of materials that are stored in their library catalogue.

From a management perspective, it is not practical to merge content of all the resources we would like our users to access into the library ILS. Libraries are not keeping up with management of the online resources they are already trying to maintain in library catalogues. They must look for ways to manage different kinds of data managed in different repositories. They are developing partnerships with content publishers, content vendors, serials agents and other libraries in the shared management of metadata needed for electronic materials. As this new management model develops libraries are letting go of the idea of each database and information repository having its own user interface. Instead, they need to be developing search interfaces that can provide users with simultaneous access to multiple metadata and content repositories at the same time.

Federated search applications demonstrate that it is possible to search vendor database content without using the associated native interface. However, library users still do the bulk of their searching using the many individual search interfaces provided with each electronic content product. In the Canadian province of Ontario, the academic computer network called "Scholars Portal" has taken an innovative approach that demonstrates another way to break the connection between vendor electronic content and vendor searcher interface (Scholars Portal, 2005). This consortium has chosen the Cambridge Scientific (CSA) web-based search platform Illumina as their primary e-journal index and full-text interface and has arranged to purchase electronic content from a variety of vendors. The consortium loads this content into a common database system, mounts it on its own servers, and uses the Illumina search interface to provide search and access services to the content. This approach to integrating resources is an alternative to purchasing a federated search application. So rather than adding a federated search interface to search a variety of resources, Scholar's Portal has consolidated content from any vendors to be searched by one interface. They have been able to do this successfully because Ontario has the high level of technological skills and resources of several large academic libraries that are not available to many other libraries. The future possibilities of this approach are great. Consolidation of e-content in a common format is a very promising development, which can make the electronic materials and their indexed metadata much more truly uniform, rather than finding a variety of means of cross searching disparate content from many vendors.

The separation between e-content database providers, federated search services and ILS/OPAC search services has been carefully maintained. Nevertheless, it too needs to be re-evaluated. Each resource provides a very similar online search and access interface. They confront very similar problems in providing search services. There is less and less usefulness to these remaining distinct and independent products. Companies in these areas have developed very similar expertise in providing search interfaces. Ebsco, CSA/Proquest and Gale have developed electronic serials search interfaces. Sirsi/Dynix and Ex Libris have long experience with search interfaces for ILS and Z39.50 systems. Serials Solutions, Muse Global and Webfeet have developed expertise in federated search tools that search both electronic content databases and ILSs. Users often judge search services by the other search services they are familiar with using, so for example, library services are often judged against the services of Amazon.com and Google.

It is equally true that the library OPAC is judged against the available features and performance of Gale Infotrac, OCLC First Search, and other popular e-journal full-text interfaces. There is a growing demand for each of these products to develop the best features of the others. Full-text database applications such as EBSCO and CSA have internal proxying facilities. A proxy server URL for a particular library can be specified within administrative setting for these database products. Search and access requests from home and remote users are automatically passed via the specified proxy server. So far, ILSs are not doing much work with proxies to develop these capabilities. e-Journal database vendors have mostly kept their search interfaces proprietary. Although the large e-content vendors have great expertise in developing search interfaces, and some of the most feature rich search tools are available, they have shown little interest in developing search tools that can search library ILSs or cross search other electronic content. ISI Web of Science has offered cross searching of other related databases for a few years now. However, Gale was the first to pursue the possibilities of cross searching and Gale released the latest version of its Power Search interface in April 2007, which can search library catalogues and cross search other vendors' electronic content.

It will be interesting to see if other vendors follow Gale in offering cross search capabilities. Some have offered basic Z39.50 interfaces, so their products might be cross-searched with library catalogues, but the functionality of such searches is limited. Many e-journal databases do not offer even basic Z39.50 searching. Link resolver products also cannot uniformly be searched via z39.50. There is obvious logic for cross searching library catalogues and link resolvers together. However, this cannot easily be done with all link resolvers using the native library catalogue search standard. Library OPAC interface software typically offers few, if any, federated search features. Federated search applications lack the capabilities to offer much library system functionality.

7

Still too many search interfaces: wrestling with old and new disintegrated applications

The problem of too many user interfaces is fundamental for libraries. The growing number of different e-journal, e-book, e-reference and OPAC interfaces present confusing access barriers for users. Federated search methods provide some limited assistance in consolidating user interfaces, but it is only a very limited solution. Each individual interface requires substantial management and configuration time, staff attention, as well as attention to coordinating with other interfaces. Creating a more unified, better-integrated information environment must be a central task for libraries. They must also work to ensure more sustainable information management. To do this, libraries need to be devoting themselves to reducing the number of interfaces they offer and avoid building new information silos. Although this seems a reasonable goal in theory, in practice libraries and content producers alike are creating new individual user interfaces and new separate information silos at a rapid rate. There are many reasons for this. In the academic world, the inclination to create new scholarly publications is hard to resist. Many new academic journals, large and small, both paid journals and open access journals are being created. With the movement away from paper serials, and recognition of the critical importance of online access, few would consider starting a journal that is not available online. Far too many journals, repositories, collections, and other online resources are still being created with little thought to how well these integrate with access resources. University presses, libraries and many other institutions and organisations are moving existing content onto the web. Sometimes they are creating new publications that must be searched with their own new proprietary interfaces. In many cases, they pay too little attention to providing federated search gateway, link resolver support, authentication tools and all of the other complex services needed to exchange information with other systems and integrate into the wider information environment.

Andrew Pace made the following comments in a recent article.

> I have long been a detractor of intense platform and interface development by content providers. While the native interface for searching publisher content has a long life ahead of it (well, maybe), I believe it is in libraries' best interest to rely on publishers for rich content and (sometimes) metadata development, not necessarily high-end technology.

> Platforms like MetaPress and HighWire Press have emerged to host content and have done so quite successfully. Other companies like Atypon Systems, which has been around since 1996, are now more visible in the library technology space. Atypon made a deal in January to co-develop a new delivery platform for JSTOR. Described as an end-to-end solution, the

Atypon platform also inserts technology throughout the publisher workflow process, handling such tasks as getting content indexed by major search engines and submitting metadata to CrossRef, PubMed and others. (Pace, 2007)

Consolidation in the electronic content industries, with its loss of intellectual diversity and competition has been a source of concern in recent years. There is no question that there are important concerns to be addressed about the autonomy of small presses and the impact on open and fair pricing as the electronic materials market becomes more and more consolidated. However, these concerns should not be an excuse for continuing to support a disintegrated and ineffective information environment.

From the information management perspective more centralisation and standardisation of online interfaces is a trend that libraries need to actively support and encourage. Large aggregated packages from vendors such as Ebsco, CSA, HighWire or Ingenta have proven their worth in greatly simplifying library management needs. The package management approach of dealing with electronic content in large groupings rather than as individual items is an essential strategy for libraries to deal with the volume of electronic content work. Consolidation of online content allows libraries and package providers to share the responsibility for maintaining metadata and other aspects of content management. Consolidation of content into larger packages and the use of a smaller number of technologically advanced online platforms such as Atypon and HighWire, also has great advantages to e-content users, providing fewer but better quality user interfaces to be searched.

As an example of a common trend, Haworth Press and Ingenta recently made the following announcement.

As part of its continuing efforts to better serve libraries and their patrons, Haworth Press has partnered with Ingenta, a leading provider of technology and services to the publishing and information industries to provide online access to full-text editions of more than 200 academic and professional Haworth journals as an additional way for librarians and others to access Haworth publications online.

Haworth will take advantage of Ingenta's global distribution and visibility by adding its journals to the IngentaConnect platform, which will co-host them with Haworth's own site. This new arrangement will allow Haworth to develop a global online content distribution system that gives libraries – and their users – concurrent electronic access when they subscribe to the print editions of the journals – at no additional cost. With each print archival subscription, libraries will be provided with an online interface that can be made available to their users – site-wide – and for distance-education programs, too.

Haworth President Bill Cohen described the arrangement as "epitomizing the "third way", which is increasingly popular among scholarly publishers who want both the autonomy and diversity of their own publication's website, but also to capitalise on the ready-made audience offered by multi-publisher platforms. Ingenta is the most established of these and, with its larger market share, was the obvious choice for us when we wanted to make our publications more widely available".

Ingenta has the unique experience of working on all types of projects for over 280 publishers worldwide and the company has created a broad network of linking relationships to assist publishers in making content widely available on the web. In addition, Ingenta has enhanced the functionality of full text by offering a comprehensive selection of reference-linking third parties. Ingenta has offices in Oxford and Bath in the UK, and in Providence, Rhode Island, and Cambridge, Massachusetts in the US.

Haworth is a major independent publisher of academic, professional and literary journals that focus on contemporary themes for contemporary audiences. Haworth's award-winning, peer-reviewed journals are edited by leaders in their fields and feature insightful writing on major subject groups and are widely indexed and abstracted by dozens of major international services, including MEDLINE, PubMed, Index Medicus, EMBASE, AHI, Magazines for Libraries, Google Scholar and the MLA International Bibliography.

About Ingenta
Founded in May 1998, Ingenta is a leading provider of technology and services to the publishing and information industries. Working initially within the academic and research sector, the company has widened its scope of operation to include other forms of online publishing, especially within the financial and business communities.

IngentaConnect   (*http://www.ingentaconnect.com*) provides access to nearly 10,000 electronic journal, book and monograph titles and nearly 30,000 fax- and Ariel-delivered publications. The site receives up to 20

> million users each month and enables users to view full
> text via subscription and through a variety of different
> payment models, including library payment accounts,
> individual subscription sales and article pay-per-view
> access. (Haworth Press, 2006)

Like many publishers, Haworth is making its content
available from a number of different platforms, while
maintaining its own proprietary platform. As an alternative
to paid hosting services, HighWire Press is an example of a
not-for-profit electronic journal service recently described
through an interview with its director, Michael A. Keller.

> Fortuitously, within 2 years of Keller's 1993 arrival on
> campus, Stanford founded HighWire Press to address
> a growing concern within academia that scientific
> societies and not-for-profit publishers would,
> individually, lack the resources and expertise to remain
> competitive in the Internet era. (Keller, in fact, calls
> digital preservation of content "the real challenge of
> the digital age".) The goals of the enterprise, which
> today serves roughly 150 client publishers, were
> twofold: "to improve the delivery of scientific research
> articles through the web and to help reputable, small-
> to medium-sized scholarly publishers make the
> transition to the online environment both efficiently
> and economically".

Although its roots lie in scientific, technical and
medical research – HighWire began with the online
production of the Journal of Biological Chemistry –
the service today hosts 361 journal titles, including
some in the social sciences. "We serve about four
million unique IP addresses a month, which generates

more than 350 million hits a month", Keller says. "If we define content sources as full-text journal articles, we're up to about 1.6 million articles". (More than 717,000 of them are available worldwide without charge.) "If we include Medline citations and abstracts, which are fully searchable within the HighWire site, the number is approaching 15 million".

But, there is more. HighWire also operates Bench Press, an XML-based manuscript submission, tracking, review and publishing system that speaks directly to HighWire's mission of "efficiency and timeliness in getting research results to press"; hosts the online edition of the Oxford English Dictionary; and manages and enforces each client publisher's subscription model "so that those who should see a particular article can and those who should not see a particular article cannot", he says.

Finally, HighWire hosts semi-annual meetings in which client publishers "discuss the features, functions and directions of scholarly publishing". "In effect", he adds, "we provide not only a standard for online journals by example, but also a forum in which the future standards are imagined, debated and decided". (Misek, 2004)

It seems increasingly obvious that most small e-journal publishers cannot provide the online interface services, authentication, federated search and link resolving offered by large publishers and aggregators. Resources such as Ingenta and HireWire provide a set of online services to both make the publishing process more effective and to integrate electronic content in the shared body of material properly. These online platforms provide a new model that allows journal publishers to concentrate on their strengths in content production, while still providing libraries with the up to date, fully featured, fully integrated search interfaces that we need to be offering our users. A growing number of libraries are strongly encouraging specialised content providers to focus their attention on producing top quality content in a timely manner, while leaving the provision of well-integrated full function search interfaces to providers who specialise in this area.

A growing number of small journal publishers, academic and not-for-profit presses are using aggregated interface tools such as Ingenta, MetaPress or HighWire to host, or provide access to their content. Quite reasonably, they focus their expertise on editorial content in their chosen subject specialty while leaving the operation of an online search interface to agencies that specialise in this area. However, many other content creators are moving in the other direction. University presses, large non-profits and smaller publishers are moving away from centralised aggregators and creating their own electronic content interfaces. Many libraries are also creating e-content interfaces. The best of these are created to support standards like OAI-PMH, (Van de Sompel *et al.*, 2003), so that their metadata can be harvested, shared and easily accessed in many ways. We often applaud and encourage libraries participating in content creation. Too often, we are still creating new silos. From a library perspective, simply making our content available on the Internet is only a partial solution. It is essential to create content repositories that can easily share information in a wide variety of ways, which use standards like OAI for making their metadata available. It is also important these repositories conform to XML-based federated search standards and make provisions for inclusion in link resolvers and other repositories, so that they can be fully searched by centralised search interfaces.

At libraries in my area new e-book offerings are coming in from a number of sources. Major book publishers such as Wiley, Springer and Elsevier are offering their own e-book collections, interfaces, etc. OCLC's NetLibrary is a prominent player, but book vendors such as Engrams and Blackwell have their own products on offer. There are many new e-book interfaces, with highly variable interoperability features and capabilities. I understand that some e-book vendors are making an effort to make their content accessible on other vendors' platforms as well as their own. Some vendors will continue to use their well-tested e-journal online interfaces to access e-books as well. Springer, Wiley and Ebsco are among the vendors who will deploy their existing e-journal interfaces to offer e-books. In terms of movement toward more unified e-content, better integration and common user interfaces, many e-book products are moving in the wrong direction so far.

It is likely that the current wide array of electronic book platforms is transitory. The e-book environment is likely to be very different in the near future. Particularly when we are buying electronic works in perpetuity, libraries need to be very concerned about the large number of incompatible and non-interoperable platforms and interfaces. Libraries should be doing everything they can to encourage e-book vendors and publishers to make their materials accessible from multiple interfaces, to make their materials interoperable, and to work toward common e-book formats in the near future.

As a manager of electronic content, I feel I must do everything I can to resist movements away from integration. Simply put, my library does not have the resources to effectively manage an enormous number of small collections and individual electronic items. Equally importantly, I have an obligation to do everything possible to limit the number of search interfaces library users must contend with. Like world carbon emissions, libraries' first effort may be simply to slow down the growth in new interfaces. Nevertheless, our longer-term goal must be to reduce the number of interfaces. In my library, this means that we are strongly favouring e-journals that can be accessed through larger aggregated packages.

Working toward better integration means clearly advocating with publishers to consolidate and standardise their interfaces whenever possible. It means holding the line ourselves on introducing new user interfaces. This is something libraries must think about as we build web portals, institutional depositories and many other online resources. Could we use another existing interface to perform this search? Could this new application or product be merged with something already in use? If we are introducing a new institutional repository, can it be built into an existing campus portal product? If the library already has a federated search application, can a federated search target be created for the new institutional repository? Can an existing Google local search incorporate the new search? Can access to the new resource be imbedded into other user interfaces that are already part of the users' workflow?

Many vendors do not seem to realise that the paradigm has shifted. It is still not uncommon for publishers to offer products that lack essential integration features such as IP validation or which make little provision for federated searching. I am approached all too often by individual journal publishers, or stand alone reference product vendors who promote the unique features of their online product(s) with little concern for how the product will integrate into the larger information environment, or be managed along with many other online resources.

7.1 CD-ROM, standalone software, and other annoying silos

CD- ROM materials were for a brief period of time an important format in libraries. This was the first media that allowed libraries to offer large amounts of digital content. From a materials management perspective, they are time consuming and cumbersome materials. In my opinion, CD-ROM and other portable media are now largely obsolete.

Other information applications require individual software to be installed and managed on many PCs that are as troublesome as CD-ROM. Portable media such as CD-ROM or DVD disks require cataloguing and storage space, as well as backup procedures. Older media such as floppy disks are particularly prone to damage. CD-ROMs are not good archival products and if these materials are held over the long term, they will have substantial preservation issues. Applications software is very commonly tied to particular computer operating systems, most commonly MS Windows. Therefore, it is not uncommon to find that a particular CD-ROM or older software product stops working when moved to a newer computer or newer version of MS Windows.

Public PCs in libraries and in college or university computer labs need an array of security measures depending on the institution's circumstances and policies on use. Security measures can all have an impact on the operation of specialised software.

There have been many thousands of CD-ROM or disk-based information products available. Business information applications are often geared to individual users and they are commonly available in disk format. Each CD-ROM disk and software package represents much more library time and effort to make available to the public than an equivalent network-based online product or book. These products require a level of individual attention that is rapidly becoming unsupportable. Software installed locally also has a number of disadvantages for users. Each software package typically has a different user interface. Sometimes the interface is even different for different editions of the same product.

As an example, my library holds 12 years of our local newspaper on annual CD-ROM disks. This newspaper is now available through a web-base newspaper service. However, these CD disks are the only available online version of the newspaper through the 1990s. The outdated user interface is not very user friendly. It does not follow popular application standards for functionality. The user interface also changed two or three times during the 10 years that the disks were being produced. So, researchers working through multiple years of these disks must contend with unexpected changes to the user interface. Only a decade ago, these CD-ROMs were a huge technological advance. The ability to search an entire year of newspaper content was a great time saver for researchers. Today, these CD-ROMs are nearly as unpopular with users as microfilm or paper indexing and abstracting volumes.

Many libraries have large collections of CD-ROMs, applications software and many other troublesome media. These will no doubt continue to serve library users for some time to come. However, it seems to me important to acknowledge that these materials represent obsolete technology and formats that are largely unloved by users, but also present substantial management costs and head aches for libraries. Libraries have not tended to take into account the media in which materials are presented. Our position has been that we have an obligation to collect materials based on usefulness and user demand rather than being concerned with inconvenient formats. While I accept that this is sometimes an unavoidable price of meeting user needs and developing a well-rounded collection, I believe that libraries should be much more active in promoting formats that support the rapid emergence of a more unified information environment.

There are several management and user services reasons for moving away from CD-ROM and other individual and stand-alone information applications. As with other electronic products where there is a proliferation of individual proprietary user interfaces, I feel an obligation to reduce the number of CD-ROM and other standalone software interfaces users must contend with and doing whatever is possible to avoid new ones.

Individual software products by their very nature are discrete silos of information. They are difficult or impossible to integrate with other information sources. Web-based, vendor-hosted search applications, with increasingly common features, now make up the majority of content sources libraries deal with. Web-based applications have a great many advantages over CD-ROM and similar products. They provide vendor-hosted and regularly updated software and content, as well as wide network availability. They routinely offer connections to library link resolvers, IP-validated user authentication, and federated search accessibility.

There is an emerging informal standardised set of integration features that users are coming to expect from all online resources. For all products that do not conform to these emerging standards, their usefulness to users must be weighed carefully against the management resources they require. e-Content products that do not conform to this informal standard present libraries with substantial problems. It is a becoming a common occurrence to hear that former print publications are becoming available in online or primarily online format only. It is remarkable how often these new online products lack basic components of the integrated electronic materials environment.

IP validation for access to electronic materials has been a fundamental part of electronic access for many years. IP access allows usage to be restricted only to computers in a library building or on a college or university campus, and requires no intervention by the library. Yet a growing number of reference book publishers are offering libraries only username and password access to their products. Libraries must keep lists of valid usernames and passwords and find secure and timely ways of providing this information to legitimate users, without providing access to unauthorised users. This requires libraries to develop methods of making usernames and passwords available to library users and monitoring and periodically changing passwords, to minimise unauthorised usage. Companies manufacturing electronic products that are primarily used in markets other than libraries are particularly prone to offering products secured by username and password, with little knowledge of the management problems this causes in large library systems. Business information tools, for financial analysis, or taxation or corporate stock research are among the products that routinely come without good IP validation methodologies. As a large part of the market for these products is in the corporate world where a few individuals at each company will access a particular online product, it is understandable that the needs of libraries are not uppermost in online business product vendors' minds.

A number of reference sources have begun delivering former print products in PDF, Excel or some similar common format, without any vendor interface and management tools, rather than provide hosted online repositories for this material. This requires libraries to develop interfaces, online repositories and long-term methods for hosting and provide access to such materials. Several vendors of former print reference products now e-mail monthly electronic files to libraries and leave it up to the library to house the material in perpetuity. A few years ago, many online products were hosted locally by libraries, both on individual user workstations and as centralised server-based applications. There are many library systems specialists, particularly at larger institutions, who still prefer this local hosting approach, because of the control it gives the library. However, most libraries have limited systems, resources and expertise. The volume of electronic materials is expanding rapidly. The overhead, in servers, expert computer technicians, network infrastructure would be far greater if libraries had not largely gone to a system where vendors are expected to host their own content and a reliable interface to it.

7.2 My library tools

User-customisable tools for organising and storing research information are a popular part of the online library environment. There are dozens of library online information products that feature individual user services for customising the user interface, saving and organising search information or research in progress. Online products such as Ebsco Host, ScienceDirect and SpringerLink all offer such "my database" services, which allow users to save previous searches and collect lists of citations they have retrieved.

Citation management applications such as Refworks, ProCite or EndNote are developing services specifically focused on collecting and organising citation material for writing academic papers. However, they also provide personal research storage services that overlap with the personalised research and storage services offered by the full-text database products. Campus portal and course management systems also provide students with personalised services for storing and organising research and other information collected. These services overlap with very popular freely available web tools for organising and sharing information such as Del.icio.us, MySpace and Facebook, which offer related services for presenting collections of personal information. Personalised space features are very popular with users. The most popular are features that allow users to share their collections of material, their views on quality, and their recommendations with others. These services provide yet another interface for users to connect directly to online content and to search or link resolver services.

The Citation Management system vendors have worked very hard with e-content vendors to ensure that there are good connections between their systems. Clearly, the success of citation management systems relies on easy movement of citation information from electronic content products into citation management systems. Library resource vendors continue to develop and market the features of their individual customisation features, while the popularity of Del.icio.us and MySpace continues to grow. However, so far, there has been little concerted effort to integrate these many user-controlled spaces. The content vendors have not made it possible to share stored research or search information between different online products or to share this information in other personal online spaces. Users are left with a large number of separate "My database", "My citation references", "My campus information", "My course materials" services each with a separate username and login password to keep track of. These cannot be connected to or shared with their MySpace, Facebook and other popular online spaces. As more and more users' services, spaces, and resources become part of the resource offerings of my library, there is an obvious need to integrate and link these services together. Users are beginning to ask, "Why can I not import my subject links or tagged items from Del.icio.us or Gmail account into my Refworks account?" and "Why can information in my database space not be merged or connected to campus portal space?"

8

Innovative interfaces, new interfaces, search services, toolbars, lookups and widgets

It is apparent that the library OPAC is being superseded, or at least challenged, by many other search interfaces. Online searchers most often begin searching Google or some other favourite search engine. They may look for books on Amazon or other online bookstores. Students are likely to be following links to information provided on course support web pages, or online courseware such as Blackboard or Web CT. Others may be regular users of a popular general full-text database such as Ebsco Academic or Gale Resource Centre, but unaware and unfamiliar with other useful tools. To address these issues, library service developers are attempting to make OPACs and other library interfaces more functional and more compelling to users. Advanced library search applications such as Endeca and Primo are the result. Other developers have undertaken to offer library search services from many new network locations, finding ways to make library services available as part of information seekers' workflow on the web. Many libraries are not relying on enticing users to come to a single library online interface, library portal or catalogue, no matter how feature-rich and enticing.

There are many innovative library projects that all aim to make connections between the results that users are finding in online searches and electronic and paper content available via their local library. A number of developers are working on automating the linkages from references to material found in web searches to full text of that material available from the searcher's local library. They are finding ways to remove steps from the user's search process. The idea is to connect users to library materials without them having to go to a library OPAC page, or check a list of available serials. The aim is to allow users to continue with their preferred web search activities while still gaining access to quality library materials and being aware of materials available to them.

John Udell's library lookup application was a web browser "bookmarklet" or software addition that automated the process of checking references found in web searching against a local library catalogue (Udell, 2002). It was one of the first applications to demonstrate that it is possible to make connections from references found on the web to library content. Book Burro is an application originally built to compare prices between several online bookstores (Book Burro, 2006). This web browser plug-in appears as an extra display box when the Amazon online bookstore website and other similar websites are searched. It automatically collects title and ISSN information about any book displayed on the screen. It then automatically searches that information against other bookstore sites, and can be configured to search a chosen library catalogue, to indicate if the book being displayed is available at the local library.

Other developers have built on the idea of automated library lookup of citations to create tools imbedded in browsers that automatically check web searches against library content in various ways. The developers of these tools are moving beyond seeing the library OPAC or e-journal databases or link resolvers as an interface that users must come to and search. Instead, they are using these resources simply as services that automated processes can search in the background, often without the user even being aware of it.

Ross Singer's OCLC prize-winning application called Umlaut is one of the most fully developed automated linking tools yet devised. Umlaut is a linking software application that works with many different online resources and services to connect users to content as seamlessly as possible. Ross Singer recently outlined the complex series of steps Umlaut takes to find appropriate links for users, and then provide them with a path to get that material.

What the Umlaut is doing

The Umlaut is actually much simpler than it appears. Each request goes through roughly the same process and none of it is terribly complicated.

1. Parse the incoming request

Every request coming into the Umlaut must either have an OpenURL ContextObject or an existing request ID (which can either be called directly: /resolve/start/17 or with the res_id argument: /resolve?res_id=17). The system then checks a local Ferret (Ruby port of Lucene) index to see if the incoming citation has been requested before.

2. Resolve standard identifiers

For dois and pmids (Eric ids, lccns, handles and oai identifiers planned), look up bib information against Crossref and Pubmed, respectively. Enhance ContextObject with data from these sites. From Pubmed, we also grab an abstract and MeSH terms (if available). The abstract will show up in the

"Description" page and the MeSH is stored to help establish "similar items".

3. Search library resources

To the Umlaut, users are associated with one or more "Institutions" (libraries) that are comprised of one or more link resolvers and one or more catalogues. For example, the institution named "Georgia Tech" contains our SFX instance, GIL and the GILUC. The institution "Emory" would have their SFX instance and EUCLID. A user that belongs to both institutions would be able view resources from all of these services.

Requests to SFX go against the SFX. The only SFX services currently supported are getFullTxt and getDocumentDelivery – when other services are enabled in SFX, they will be added to the Umlaut.

To facilitate better results from our collection, we export the bib records out of Voyager and index them with Indexdata's Zebra.

With the MODS records out of the OPAC, we enhance the ContextObject (much like above), mainly by adding things such as publisher and publication (or ISxN, if missing).

A local web service is also called to grab some extra information from SFX that is not accessible via SFX application programming interface (API). If the citation has an ISSN, a request is sent to a local database (of data extracted from SFX reports) with the argument "issn". (example) The server returns a JSON response with the SFX Object ID, Title, ISSN, the providers and their coverages, the proprietary subject headings that SFX has assigned to the journal, and then a list of the journal titles that share the most number of similar subjects sorted descending by clickthroughs in the last month.

4. Search Yahoo! and Google with the article/item title, author and year
Using the Google and Yahoo! APIs, we send searches using the article title (or journal/book title if no article title) and the author name (or as much of the author's name as we have). Yahoo! allows you to scope your queries with a "context", so if there is a date in the citation, we use that for context. Yahoo! allows a max of 50 search results. I have not figured Google out, really. We are using Ruby/Google.

5. Search Amazon for item if it has an ISBN
With the ISBN, we search the Amazon API and grab everything that seems pertinent. We grab the description (which will appear on the description page), the "library subjects" they assign to items, cover images, and the "similar items". We also grab the link to the page so that the user has the option to search inside the book (although whether or not that is available is not in the API). The medium sized cover image goes in the citation display. The similar items are used in the "get more like this" screen and the subjects are stored for our own recommender service.

6. Determine the "Relevant" items from the Yahoogle searches
Ah... "relevant". This is a bit tricky and we are taking a very brain-dead approach to this. First, we have

created a "white list" of things that "probably have something to do with scholarly citations". What we have done is taken the Registry of OpenAccess Repositories and added arXiv.org, Citeseer, Citebase, Open WorldCat, NASA, SMARTech, etc. For some of these sites we have written handlers to do extra things (Open WorldCat puts a "highlighted link", arXiv.org/Citebase/Citeseer appear as full-text targets, SMARTech will when repoMan is rewritten).

Then we run every link that was found by Yahoo! and Google and run it through EzProxy. If EzProxy wants to proxy the link, we assume it is relevant in some way (this has varying results, sometimes it is just a link to IngentaConnect for an article that cites the requested citation or something).

7. Display the results
At this point, the user has waited long enough. We still have more information to gather, but we will do that in the background (especially as these are the slow services). The "start screen" attempts to resemble a traditional link resolver menu as much as possible. We display the full-text targets first (including targets such as arXiv.org, Citeseer, Citebase, etc.), followed by any print sources the user has access to. We also show the "relevant" web search results on this screen. You will find a lot of good stuff in there, actually. It is a good means to get to ACM and IEEE materials that fall outside OPAC/SFX knowledgebase.

On the right, we have the context menu based on the citation in question. Options will be available for description?, table of contents?, related titles?, get more like this?, web search results? and session history?

Below that, are highlighted links?. These might be links to the record in Open WorldCat, Amazon, a citation list in Citeseer, etc. They do not currently, but should, change depending on the screen that is being viewed.

When the page is rendered, a JavaScript function calls back to the umlaut to start doing the background processes. This way the user is unaffected. (Singer, 2006)

Umlaut goes beyond simply looking up references in an ILS and link resolver. It attempts to overcome shortcomings in available metadata by checking several sources to provide addition identifying information. Umlaut uses multiple library ILS and link resolvers as well as other resources including Amazon, Crossref and PubMed as information services to aid it in the identification and linking process.

A growing number of libraries are building library catalogue searches and full-text database searches into the toolbar for the users' web browser. Internet Explorer, Firefox and the Google Toolbar for web browsers all now have built-in capabilities for adding customised searches to the toolbar. These toolbar products work best with library search tools that can be readily searched with search parameters passed via URL. Not all full-text database tools, OPACs and federated search tools can be easily searched this way. However, for the ones that can, it is now easy for libraries to allow users to search without having to go to an OPAC or online database search pages. A number of libraries have customised their own browser toolbar search applications. However, Virginia Tech has developed LibX, one of the most sophisticated toolbar products. LibX combines toolbar search features with the integrated library lookup capabilities similar to those of Umlaut.

Annette Bailey and Godmar Back, the developers of LibX, described its intentions and capabilities in a recent article:

> LibX, [is] a Firefox extension that provides users with direct access to library resources from anywhere on the web. LibX is seamlessly integrated into the user's browser. It consists of multiple components. A toolbar component allows the user to construct direct searches against their library's OPAC without having to navigate to the OPAC search interface pages. A context menu component allows a user to quickly construct searches from text selected on any web page, such as a book title or international standard book number (ISBN) displayed on a page. A third component gives access to the library's OpenURL linking server (Van de Sompel et al., 2001). Users can select article references found on any web page and with a few mouse clicks retrieve an accessible copy of the article being cited. A fourth component embeds cues into web pages the user visits. These cues alert the user to library resources that are related to the content of the page. For instance, a cue on a book review page can link directly to the library catalogue entry for the book being discussed. (Bailey and Back, 2006)

Bailey and Black also describe how LibX uses the common capabilities of HTML to construct URL strings that pass search requests to the library ILS. Rather than using any standardised process and information exchange interface, they find themselves customising URL strings that will be recognised by particular ILSs. The development of LibX has continued since this article was written. An Internet Explorer version is now available. Tools for local customisation of LibX have been added, and it now supports a wider selection of ILSs. The authors continue on:

OPAC searching
Approach and implementation
LibX users can initiate OPAC searches either from the toolbar or from the context menu without having to navigate to the web page hosting the OPAC interface. To implement this access, we examined how the OPAC is accessed as a web service.

Most OPACs use the representational state transfer model (REST) (Fielding, 2000). In this model, all data that is required to describe a query is transmitted as part of an URL. A hypertext transfer protocol (HTTP) GET request is sent to the server, which then decodes the request, performs the search and returns the results. Some OPACs use POST requests by default, which can typically be converted into equivalent GET requests.

Since we did not have access to the OPAC server, we needed to reverse-engineer the format of the GET requests. We systematically ran a set of queries with different search options from the library's OPAC page and noted the URLs that resulted. These included basic searches by title, keyword, author, etc. as well as advanced searches with logical operators. We also examined the forms included in those pages using Firefox's built-in page information dialog. When the user initiates a search from LibX, JavaScript code constructs a URL based on the user's search terms and options. We have found this approach to be simple and reliable even for advanced searches containing multiple search options and terms. (Bailey and Back, 2006)

Similar to Umlout, LibX looks to centralised services on the web to gather information needed to link users search results to available library content as Bailey and Back describe it.

xISBN integration

In some cases, books are available under more than a single ISBN. To help the user find a copy that is held by the library, we included an option for the user to retrieve sets of ISBNs from OCLC's xISBN service. This service allows users to search for ISBNs that are related to a given ISBN. These sets of ISBNs were created by data-mining OCLC's Worldcat catalogue. For instance, the ISBN of a book's hardcover edition is related to the ISBN of the same book's paperback edition. This service allows the user to find a book even if the library holds a version of the book that has a different ISBN than the ISBN the user was searching for. (Bailey and Back, 2006)

Because link resolvers use the OpenURL standard for describing materials, LibX can use this standard for constructing search queries to be passed to a link resolver.

OpenURL searches

LibX allows users to formulate and execute queries against their library's OpenURL linking server. Such queries can be constructed from the search fields provided in the toolbar, or from selected text on the page a user is currently visiting.

If the OpenURL is constructed from input a user entered into the toolbar's search fields, we map the search fields to the metatags OpenURL 0.1 supports: for instance, the Title: field is mapped to title, the Author: field is mapped to the aulast and aufirst metatag, the Article Title: field is mapped to an atitle metatag, and so on.

OpenURL searches can also be initiated directly from a selection on a page: LibX recognizes when the user selects text that forms a valid international standard serials number (ISSN) or document object identifier (DOI), using the same technique described earlier for ISBNs. In these cases, we add entries to the context menu, which, when activated, will construct and initiate OpenURL queries based on either the ISSN metatag or via the global identifier syntax (id = doi: 10/...). (Bailey and Back, 2006)

LibX also looks to online resources such as Google Scholar to collect the information needed to track down references users may encounter.

Search via Google Scholar

The method described in the previous section has a drawback: a user may not know all of the information that is necessary for a linking server to find the referenced resource. For instance, a user might know only the article title, but a particular linking server might require that an OpenURL that carries the article genre contain at least a journal title or an ISSN. Even if the ISSN or journal title were known, a linking server may not have access to an index of article titles for a particular journal, which would then require the user to specify volume, part and year of an article they are seeking. For these reasons, it is desirable that an OpenURL contain as many metatags as possible. If a global identifier such as a DOI is known, including it in the OpenURL vastly increases the chance that a particular linking server implementation will be able to resolve the OpenURL and find the document or resource.

LibX automates the process of finding an OpenURL that has a high likelihood of being successfully resolved. To this end, we use the Google Scholar search engine as a hidden backend. We submit search terms to Scholar and harvest the OpenURLs it returns. For the user, this facility can make finding an article from an unlinked reference encountered on a web page as simple as selecting all or parts of the reference and activating the Search via Scholar search. The search can be activated either through the context menu, or by dragging and dropping the selection onto the "Scholar" button. The drag-and-drop feature is particularly useful when finding citations in portable document format (PDF) files that are viewed from inside browser plug-ins such as acrobat reader.

The Search via Scholar feature uses a heuristics that is based on the cosine similarity measure to identify whether Scholar found the item for which the user searched. If the heuristics determines that the item was found and Scholar provided an OpenURL for the result, the user is taken directly to the linking server. If we are unable to find the article, we simply open the Scholar results page in a browser tab and rely on the user to adjust their search terms manually. (Bailey and Back, 2006)

Linking tools such as Umlaut or LibX can undertake complex sets of interactions between different systems to locate available content for users. They can improve searches by automatically checking the OCLC xISSN service to seek alternate ISSN numbers for the same work or seek additional citation information from sources such as PubMed, Cross-Ref and Google Scholar. They have the interactive capability to collect and cross check information from several different sources and respond differently depending on the information they have available to them. These tools show the real possibilities to apply artificial intelligence to the problems of routing online searchers to the information materials they are seeking.

These applications do an impressive amount of information exchange between different systems. When done successfully, this work is entirely invisible to library users. Libraries must expect to see this kind of integration be built into primary link resolving software in the near future. This large amount of interaction and information exchange between different systems is dependent first on there being reliable automated means for requesting information from different systems and reliable automated means of receiving and processing the results. These systems use a variety of information interchange standards, particular OpenURL. However, all too often they rely on the ability to customise the common features of HTML and related web publishing features to exchange information. These systems also depend for success on sufficiently detailed, entirely accurate and up-to-date metadata being available on every system involved in the integration. Accurate lists of serials titles, accurate holdings information, in library ILS and in link resolver knowledgebases, up-to-date title change information are essential to allow seamless connections to content for users.

These new automated and integrated linking tools place new demands on library materials management. They move well beyond the old model of the library catalogue as a single user interface and single repository of metadata about locally-held materials. Instead, these interactive linking tools can use multiple ILS, link resolvers and other more global repositories as distributed services that work together to respond to users' information needs.

8.1 User perceptions of broken

In my experience, any barrier to a successfully completed search and access transaction is simply taken as a broken system and this includes barriers intentionally built in to the system. My university has provided excellent wireless Internet access across the campus. We made a conscious decision not to include printing capabilities, for various security and technical reasons. This seemed a reasonable compromise to the people implementing wireless services. However, it is not viewed as an understandable limit by students; it is simply seen as a failed, broken, or malfunctioning system.

Students with whom I speak see citation references found in indexing and abstracting databases where there is no link to full text or information about availability in the same light. Indexing tools that provide references only have been a central part of library resources for many years. It was understood that users of these indexes have training from library staff to understand that once citations are found in an index, they will have to pursue the journal or book referred to in the index citation by looking it up in another source, most often the library catalogue. This interrupted process of searching first for likely reference citations and then checking to see if the cited content is available, is a basic part of the research process, as libraries have implemented it. Today's online searchers simply see this interrupted multi-step process as broken. They know that full text is available from many online sources. They also expect to see working resolver links to take them to full text in other sources and, if this is not possible, they expect to be told when full text is not available from their local library and to be given information on how they may obtain the needed material.

Our complex integrated systems thus succeed or fail on their weakest link. A federated search might integrate searching 10 databases. It then links the results in most cases to electronic full text via a link resolver, and to paper full text via the library OPAC. If full text is not available, the system might provide a document delivery form to request items from other libraries. If any of the 14 separate online systems involved in this process fails to perform, users will view the process as malfunctioning. This high standard of functionality applies equally to simple data errors in all of our automated systems. If the system indicates that particular journal issues are available and they are in fact not available, if the database says the library holds an item when it does not, users simply view the system as broken. It is of course, remarkable how well and how often the integrated processes we are building work successfully.

9

End-to-end integration and a seamless user experience

A growing number of libraries are building online search interfaces that combine federated search tools, link resolvers and the library catalogue along with other components to create highly integrated end-to-end search and retrieval applications.

The idea behind end-to-end integration is simply that users should be able to move from looking for relevant materials to locating and getting the material, in a single seamless process. Online searchers are expecting a seamless process from search to materials. End-to-end integration simply fixes what are perceived to be broken search services in many online searchers' eyes, and closes the gaps between user expectations and what our systems often currently deliver. Each user search will usually include several databases and library catalogues. A user may be directed to paper materials in libraries or available online materials. He or she may also be directed to order materials that can be rapidly delivered by other libraries or via document delivery. The emphasis is on making the process more seamless and making the interaction between many diverse library systems invisible to the end user.

It seems a basic principle that when searchers find a reference using any search tool, be it Google or

PsychArticles, that what they are looking for is immediate access to the full text of the document discovered. If possible, they would like a button to push that says "full text". The popular journal databases often offer several links to a PDF copy of the article, as well as a link to a web version of the article. Searchers do not care if a document they are seeking appears in the database they are searching or some other database, as long as the material is accessible to their library. If the document is not immediately available online, searchers need several access questions answered as directly as possible. They need to know if the item is available in their library. If so, they need to know the call number and directions to find the document. They need to know if an item is available at a nearby library or if the item can be quickly delivered via some sort of document delivery. If so, they need to be led through the procedure for requesting the item. They may need to identify themselves, or fill out a form, and they need information on how, when and where they may pick the item up, or have the item delivered to them. All of our materials management efforts are directed at providing searchers with the information they need to complete the search and material retrieval process. New seamless user interfaces attempt to lead information seekers through one continuous, uninterrupted process, from selection of the correct information resource to the search query, and then on to available full text.

Link resolving has been a major step forward in connecting searchers to materials they are seeking, but it does not make the research process seamless and can present searchers with extra complexities. The typical link resolver offers the online searcher a link resolver button that provides the users with a page of information. It shows links to the available e-journal websites or databases where full text to the article in question is available. It may offer links to table of contents for the journal, whether or not full text is available. The link resolver display can offer a link to look up the journal in the local library ILS, to see if paper holdings might be available. Users of the link resolver must determine which links on the resolver page to click on. Often the link resolver will provide assistance in making further progress with the search for full text, but it is not always clear to the user. Users must infer certain information from the link resolver, such as whether electronic full text is available for a particular journal reference or if a paper copy of the article is available.

Researchers studying users' behaviour have found that users often do not understand the steps and processes involved in searching for library materials. Several research studies have shown that even with link resolving and federated search tools, users remained confused about the search process and the correct path to follow to search for and retrieve materials they need for their research. Users often do not understand the connections between different e-journal databases, the library catalogue and document delivery applications (Bowen, 2004). These researchers found that students did not readily understand the connection between finding a reference in an indexing database, or a web search engine, and finding the full-text article for that reference. Searchers should not need to concern themselves with the diverse e-content vendors and publishers that are the sources of electronic content they find in their searches or concern themselves with the technical methods used to present information to them.

Link resolving and federated searching were created to simplify the information search and retrieval process. They have been very successful and powerful tools, but to many users they add more components to an already confusing information environment. User testing tends to show, as

Gail Herrera has noted, that library online services are often "unintentionally elaborate mazes" and that "users become lost in a quagmire of choices" (Herrera, 2007).

Researchers at the University of Rochester have focused on usability testing library catalogues and other online systems such as link resolving. They have found in several studies that users are often confused by library search tools. Jennifer Bowen, Head of Cataloguing at Rochester, characterised libraries' attempts to provide search access to electronic serials as "serial failure". She wrote that "In 1997, students searching for articles from the libraries' home page were required to intuit that their first step was to click on the button labeled databases, a conceptual leap that virtually no students made" (Bowen, 2004).

In their presentation "Metadata that supports real user needs", Jennifer Bowen and David Lindahl outlined some of the difficulties that students encountered using library online search tools. Their usability testing found that students were unclear about many parts of the search processes they encountered in libraries. To begin with, students often did not know that they needed to use an online index or database to look for materials. They often do not have the information or the skills to select a useful database for their subject. Students were often unclear about what they were searching; was it locally available materials, online journal articles or freely available materials on the web? They were reluctant to make choices between different sources. Then having found references, students were unclear as to what process to follow to access different kinds of materials. These include online articles, books and materials in a digital repository and materials available via document delivery. Students had particular problems getting to full text. They did not find it clear from interface screens if the items they needed were available online or not. They found the paths from search results to linked full text or methods of content access required too many page clicks and that the linking information was prone to error. Too often, material that appeared to be available turned out not to be available. Bowen and Lindahl pointed out the importance of user centred design and usability testing in order to get the best results from metasearch technology (Lindahl and Bowen, 2005).

A growing number of academic libraries are developing systems that tie the diverse components of the search process together into one seamless operation. The search of multiple journal databases is merged with a check of the link resolver and library catalogue for possible full text. If full text is available, the user is presented with a button to retrieve it. If full text is not available, then the user is told this and presented with options for ordering the material from a document delivery source. The aim of these systems is to present the user with an interface that leads them end-to-end through the process of selecting online places to search; formulating and performing the search itself, and then being directed from the search results to available full text in one smooth, uninterrupted series of steps.

Based on their extensive user testing, the University of Rochester developed a system they called GUF (getting users to full text). They made the challenge of "two clicks to full text" an objective of this system. They developed a highly integrated library search interface that hides the complexities of the linking process from users. It is simple and well organised enough so that users can move from search results to available full-text materials in two clicks. (Lindahl and Suszczynski, 2005) The California State University at San Marcos developed a similar library integrated library interface called Xerxes. This interface is customised using the MetaLib federated search application, the SFX link resolver and other components. California State University system has built on Xerxes to develop their Unified Information Access System (UIAS) which now includes the Iliad inter-library loan management system (Pollard, 2005).

The University of Rochester is continuing its work in creating highly integrated library systems. In 2005, the University began a multi-year development project funded in part by the Carnegie Mellon Foundation. Researchers set out to build what they have called the Extensible Library catalogue or XC. Library director David Lindahl described the project in a recent interview. He noted "There is no shortage of forward thinking project work in this area, and we hope to leverage what has been done and set up a broad but effective collaboration to build XC" (Bell, 2006).

What follows is the text of the interview, written in question and answer style:

What was the original impetus for this new project?

Mainly a desire to improve on existing cataloging systems or something else?

The XC project will have the following goals.

- To design a catalog that would deal with other metadata formats beyond MARC, and that would have an architecture that could evolve with future standards.

- To address the long list of known usability issues that exist with current web OPAC components of most major integrated library systems.

- To not build an entire ILS, but to focus on the metadata platform and the user interface. XC would interoperate with any existing ILS.

- To leverage our experience in work-practice study methodology to uncover unmet user needs related to library catalog functionality, and to address those needs.

Can you describe, for the non-techies among us, just what exactly an extensible catalog is (or would be)?

- XC will be a single entry point into all of the resources (print and electronic) that a library has to offer. It will be easy to learn and powerful for experienced users. No training will be necessary, and the software will deliver initial results in one click.

- XC incorporates a metadata infrastructure that would support the full range of metadata standards. This would allow libraries to connect XC with their library webpages, digital and institutional repositories, and subscription databases. As libraries move forward and offer new types of repositories, they continue to create new silos of information with separate interfaces. XC will consolidate these disparate systems with appropriately integrated user interface(s).

- The XC will be easy to download and install in any library. We will be developing a set of software requirements over the next year.

Is it possible this project could result in a different type of OPAC? If so, can you please describe that OPAC?

- A goal of XC is to develop a new type of OPAC. We hope that the end result will be a software system that works alongside an existing

ILS/OPAC, and offers an alternative to the built-in web interface.

- We want the XC to be extensible, so that it can handle new types of metadata, we want other libraries to add functionality to the XC (open-source), we want to have APIs into all the functionality to enable libraries to experiment and create a range of user-interfaces, not just one, and then work with users and evolve with them.

- Libraries have invested a great deal of their resources in creating and maintaining metadata, but ILS software does not allow the average user to take advantage of that metadata. We hoped that a more powerful search interface would help our patrons to become more successful with finding and using library resources.

- Instead of building a search interface that burdens the user with complex language, multiple search boxes, cryptic choices and overwhelming result sets, XC will offer an interface that anyone can use without training.

- The user interface will work with users to guide them to precise, comprehensive results. This might include a single search box that would search across resources that are today found in the catalog, digital repository and subscription databases. The interface might check spelling, decrypt journal title abbreviations, connect expressions and manifestations with their respective works, and offer faceted browsing of result sets to interactively guide users to appropriate results.

(Bell, 2006)

The ambitious goals of the Extensible Library Catalogue project bring together several related integrating efforts. It aims to closely integrate ILSs with other library systems. But it is clearly intended to be a stand-alone interface system that is independent of any particular ILS or link resolver. It will provide enhancements to library catalogue search capabilities, such as faceted searching, while attempting to truly merge multiple searches with a single interface. It will present users with a seamless end-to-end process from search to linking to access.

Many libraries have now built working versions, prototypes or only promising portions of new expanded and enhanced search tools or seamlessly integrated interfaces. They offer users simpler, more convenient and intuitive ways to find and access library materials.

The great improvements that can be made to our current OPACs and user interfaces have been clearly demonstrated. Seamless interfaces such as the California State University Unified Information Access System or Rochester's XC use automated linking and look up features similar to tools such as Umlaut and LibX. These innovative interfaces demonstrate capabilities that can transform the search and access experience for most library users. If Rochester succeeds in developing the capabilities they envision for XC and make this available as an open source application, the library community will have a powerful new tool set.

Unfortunately, so far the tools that libraries need to provide seamless access to their resources or a full range of search capabilities cannot be purchased from any single vendor. The necessary management and integration tools are not available as standard features of any ILS, link resolver application or federated search software. The interaction that is required between many different library systems remains complex. Libraries have had to substantially customise and often improvise to create innovative systems. Therefore, we clearly have a new model for library user interfaces, but the tools to fully realise this new model are not yet available to most libraries.

Innovative search interfaces also transform the way libraries look at our materials management systems and what we expect from these systems. The ability to supply the information needed by lookup linking, extended search and other integration services should be a focus of attention. Libraries and their systems vendors need to see their systems as service providers to multiple other systems and interfaces. They must work to develop the information interchange capabilities of each system. Libraries also need to be working to collect or access new kinds of information such as persistent URLs or related ISBN information needed to create a more seamless user experience.

10

Net size, bigger and better partnerships, and getting others to share the work

The development of a worldwide integrated information environment is of course, far bigger than libraries. So far, Internet companies such as Amazon, Google and Yahoo!, and software companies such as Microsoft and Adobe have been at the forefront of this revolution. Many libraries have felt that they could only sit on the sidelines and react to events in the information environment. But projects such as Crossref, Open WorldCat and book digitisation projects including Google's, show that libraries can have a vital role.

The World Wide Web as it has developed so far remains disorganised and un-coordinated. There is an enormous opportunity for libraries to apply their skills at organising and coordinating information, and their basic service and access values to a great many problems of the Internet. But libraries must first realise that the tool set we have developed in the past for coordinating and organising information is largely ineffective in dealing with the volume, diversity and volatility of the materials on the web. There is a pressing need and more or less unlimited opportunities to develop global tools to coordinate online information.

Even as libraries are working to improve their local

online systems, and make connections between them, there are great possibilities to integrate our services at the global network level. Lorcan Dempsey was recently quoted commenting on the possibilities for creating centralised web-based services for libraries. An excerpt from the interview follows:

> In the 1970s, libraries moved cataloging and inter-library loan to the network level with OCLC online services, in which libraries combine to create value that could not be achieved at the institutional level. The community is exploring how to do this with virtual reference in QuestionPoint. The challenge moving forward is to identify other places where libraries will benefit from this model, says Lorcan Dempsey, OCLC Vice President.

> "What has happened is that the network has come 'inside', it has entered our experiences", Dempsey says. "It has changed forever what is possible. It is the medium that realizes workflow and process and it requires a different way of thinking and working".

> Dempsey says that many of the issues facing libraries are about working in pre-network environments where things are done many times, redundantly and in fragmented ways. Think of metasearch, he says, where the fragmentation caused by legacy technology and business practices is inefficient and ineffective. Google Scholar is one approach to moving this issue to the network level.

> "Things are moving up, moving to the network level. This is the burden of the long tail argument; it is at the

root of many of the major forces that are changing our world".

In the new network environment, libraries need to identify services that go beyond a single institution and remove redundancy, build capacity and allow for collective activity. Think about preservation, storage, tools for analysis, reformatting, transformation, data duration – even a storage framework and logistical network for physical collections, Dempsey says. It simply does not make sense to tackle these with institution-level development. It is expensive and functionally suboptimal.

"We need to move common solutions to the network level, allowing libraries to concentrate on creating local value for their students and scholars rather than redundantly working on everyone's problems". (Storey, 2006)

Libraries have a long history of creating shared resources such as union catalogues. Our processes, from copy cataloguing to consortium purchasing, are highly cooperative. Libraries continue to work hard to reduce the obvious amount of duplication in our collection of materials management metadata. As I have been describing, libraries are already relying on systems of distributed centralised online metadata repositories to manage and organise the materials we make available.

Large vendor-hosted resources including major full-text aggregators such as Gale InfoTrac or EbscoHost are important global repositories of electronic serials information. The libraries that use any of these electronic content services look to them to provide electronic serials information that includes title lists, persistent URLs and often MARC records. These e-serials vendors must maintain detailed information about the e-journal packages of their competitors as well as their own holdings. Libraries with limited resources must rely on these sources of information rather than maintaining their own metadata. For a large number of smaller libraries and libraries that do not maintain a link resolver or electronic serials information in their ILS, vendor-hosted e-content databases are their only repository of electronic serials information.

In the same way, link resolvers are another important example of network-wide central metadata repositories. Each link resolver company maintains extensive repositories of title lists, URL linking, and other metadata. Many libraries are coming to see their link resolver as a parallel and complementary source of metadata to their ILS. But the link resolver knowledgebase is a centralised repository maintained by the resolver vendor and shared by all libraries using that link resolver company.

Serials agent systems maintained by companies such as Ebsco, Swetts and Blackwell are becoming another central resource upon which libraries are relying. Serials agent companies must maintain vast amounts of information about available serials. They must have an accurate and up to date record of the multiple URLs associated with any individual serial, as well as title change information, different sources of availability for each journal, listings of ISSN numbers for both paper and electronic versions of serials, as well as licence provisions and registration processes. We must assume that serials agents are working with serials publishers to collect this information centrally in standardised forms, rather than each serials agent developing separate proprietary standards and processes with vendors. Serials vendors maintain records for the materials that libraries purchase and license.

There is an obvious case for developing automated means of moving information about library serials holdings directly from serials agent systems into library ERM systems, or ILSs. There are several efforts such as Onyx for Serials moving in this direction but these are not yet widely available. Serials agents are providing a growing range of services, at least to their clients, for accessing their important central repositories of information. But the methods for viewing, editing and extracting this information are manual. It is left to individual libraries to input information provided by their serials agent into other library systems. Serials vendors make this information freely available to libraries using their purchasing services. It is very possible to develop lookup type web services for serials agent systems. Serials agent systems contain much of the information provided by link resolvers, with considerably more detail. They also duplicate information being collected by individual electronic content databases.

The electronic content vendors, link resolver companies and serials agents must maintain sophisticated processes between them to share ever-changing metadata about their electronic offerings. The Crossref shared serials link information service, developed by electronic publishers as well as libraries, shows the possibilities for an open and centralised network level service for serials linking information. However, Crossref has not been as comprehensive as it needs to be, and the serials metadata that it maintains is somewhat limited. Despite the range of centralised vendor services that are collecting information about electronic content, none of these services provides a complete or authoritative source for this information. Many libraries still find that they must do as the University of New Brunswick does, and maintain their own information on their electronic serials holdings. These libraries put considerable staff time into keeping this information up to date as journal, title, holdings and URL information changes month by month.

e-Content vendors and service providers must maintain accurate, detailed and up-to-date electronic content information in order to carry on their business dealings with libraries. It seems reasonable to ask every publisher of e-content to provide libraries with accessibility information on request. Again, libraries should be looking to have this information available in centralised and freely available online repositories, which expand on the promise of the Crossref online service.

The UK Serials Group released a report in May 2007 exploring the issues affecting link resolving (Culling, 2007). One of its major recommendations is to create an international organisation to oversee the collection and quality control of link resolver information, with a centralised metadata repository. This organisation would be based on the model of the COUNTER (Counting Online Usage of NeTworked Electronic Resources) organisation for e-content database statistics.

It is also possible to expect centrally reposited information to be available through automated online services, so that library repositories like ILSs and knowledgebases can be populated through automated exchange of information with centralised vendor information repositories. The electronic content industry has the advantage of economies of scale over individual libraries in maintaining common information on their products, and then adjusting this information as needed for individual libraries. Libraries need to look to the content industry to work together to build on existing repository services. It seems only a mater of time before electronic serials information resources are merged or cross-linked into a single system for providing electronic journal metadata.

Another example of transition to the network level is the rapid movement of library technology from local management to vendor hosting. Libraries first looked to vendors to manage the server resources of electronic content databases. A growing number of libraries are looking to vendors to centrally manage their link resolvers, federated search applications and even library ILSs. Many libraries store their serials information in a link resolver knowledgebase centrally hosted by Serials Solutions or Ebsco. They store information about their books in a local catalogue, but book cover images are extracted on the fly as needed from a centralised repository maintained by Syndetics Solutions. Thus, libraries are already using network-wide distributed systems to manage electronic materials. The networked systems that have evolved so far just show the scope and possibilities for further development.

We see a remarkable number of centralised repositories and shared information resources being developed on the Internet. The Open WorldCat library catalogue is an obvious example of the possibilities for globalising services for libraries and services offered by libraries. In 2004, OCLC partnered with Google and Yahoo! to make indexing for many millions of book records available for search on the Internet, and link those records back to the libraries that hold the books. Open WorldCat has been a major step forward in service for libraries. It exposes library holding to the world's Internet searchers. Open WorldCat raises at least the conceptual possibility of a central library catalogue replacing individual library catalogues. OCLC and several library partners are continuing to explore the possibilities of Open WorldCat by creating local World Cat versions of individual libraries (OCLC, 2007). There has so far been little suggestion that Open WorldCat or other global repositories can or should replace local library catalogues. As long as libraries maintain large physical collections of materials and lend those materials, they will have need for sophisticated inventory control of their local materials. But this does not mean that complete bibliographic descriptions of each book or URLs for each online item, must be duplicated in each library catalogue. Distributed linking methods offer many possibilities for holding local inventory and subject access information in local databases, while looking to central networked repositories of common information including basic bibliographic description. Distributed linking and the storage of metadata in multiple networked repositories mean that libraries no longer need to be tied to the model of one central and independent catalogue as the sole repository for information about each library's offerings.

The Google Books project demonstrates even more far-reaching possibilities for moving library services to the network. Libraries have just begun to consider the implications of having all published books fully indexed and searchable on the World Wide Web. It also seems reasonable to conceive of a world in which every published journal is indexed and searchable on the World Wide Web. It seems reasonable to anticipate that those journals will be available to be browsed, sorted and examined from a single list on the web. On today's Internet a great deal of journal material is indexed but there is no way of knowing what is there or not there. It is easy to conceptualise global, networked approaches to managing what are currently considered to be library materials. Distributed searching and linking, network repositories and widespread web indexing offer possible approaches that go well beyond the methods that libraries use today. Even with the most efficient current methods, in aggregate libraries, information vendors and publishers spend many millions duplicating library cataloguing information and various kinds of metadata record keeping. Network-wide centralised information repositories offer an obvious opportunity to reduce these costs. Centralised metadata repositories are going to be an important part of libraries' future efforts. Libraries have an opportunity to build on services such as Crossref and Open WorldCat, and leverage the work of subscription agents and link resolver companies to develop central repositories for much of the metadata that libraries are currently collecting locally.

Reference information sources have particular potential for being moved to the network level. There is nothing new about global reference information sources. They have been a central feature of library reference for a long time. Reference publishing serves to provide centralised directory and indexing services that individual libraries could not attempt to maintain on their own. We look to globally available paper resources like Sociological Abstracts or Ulrichs Serials Index to provide authoritative and comprehensive coverage of the materials beyond the scope that any single library could maintain individually. The approach was to offer many copies of common reference volumes such as encyclopaedias, yearbooks and directories accessible from local libraries. This multiple duplication of information services was the only effective method libraries and publishers had for distributing reference information. In the same way, we maintain duplicate sets of resource information for managing library materials, e.g. *Books in Print* or Library of Congress subject heading directories. It is now possible to aggregate, at a global level, much of the reference information that libraries at one time collected and made available individually. It is also possible to collect globally much of the metadata and materials management information that libraries still collect locally. The Internet simply provides new possibilities, new dimensions and broader access to the same kind of central reference repositories.

Worldwide reference resources such as Google Maps or Wikipedia are the obvious examples of the many resources that demonstrate the possibilities for aggregating reference information at the global network level. Several important US Government reference sources have led the way for global subject authoritative reference resources. The Educational Resources Information Clearing House (ERIC) and the National Library of Medicine (Medline) database are important examples. There are a growing number of examples of resources that once relied on libraries as exclusive distributors, which can now be directly distributed via the World Wide Web. In Canada, the library deposit programs for government documents are being overtaken by release of most government documents in digital form on the World Wide Web. The Canadian Federal Government has made a concerted effort to make government materials freely web accessible. Government agencies around the world are moving in a similar way to make former paper publications freely available in PDF or similar formats. The United States National Technical Information Service (NTIS), The Stationary Office (TSO) of the UK and Statistics Canada are examples of major government online repositories, which are making large amounts of material available via the Internet that would formerly have been stewarded by libraries. Huge collections of material that were formerly only available through libraries are now available to users directly online. This is an important step forward for information access, although libraries often struggle to adjust to this disintermediation.

From a materials management perspective, new

collections of freely available materials such as government documents present some difficult problems. Libraries must make decisions about what freely available materials to add to library catalogues. Many of these materials were only selectively added to library catalogues in paper form. But a much greater volume of material than would have formerly been managed by libraries is now being made freely available. There is enough of this material to overwhelm most libraries' cataloguing capabilities. Libraries must question the effectiveness of cataloguing large bodies of material that can be readily located by Google or Yahoo!. But the current circumstance where materials may be randomly located on the World Wide Web does not provide consistent or reliable access. Many libraries are being tempted to improve the visibility and accessibility of government materials and other quality materials on the web by attempting to catalogue them; an insurmountable and unsustainable task. Instead, we must be looking to large producers of freely available material, such as government agencies, to provide more orderly indexing and metadata access to their materials and better centralised aggregation of metadata for these materials.

There are many possibilities for creating global encyclopaedic reference resources that rival and exceed what has been done so far. Wikipedia and Amazon have offered models for more specific and authoritative information resources, which use the power of the web and the work of many practitioners, to create comprehensive repositories on particular topics. Shared centralised resources offer much more efficient and lower cost methods for aggregating information, than former paper publishing methods. Examples such as the Stanford Encyclopedia of Philosophy International Association (SEPIA, 2007) demonstrate that there are unlimited opportunities to create free or inexpensive comprehensive repositories in hundreds of specialised disciplines. It is easy to envision most library reference volumes, from key directories to encyclopaedias, being offered as online sources. Many libraries have recognised the possibilities of centralised reference resources and are becoming involved in global efforts to develop network-wide resources. Reference book publishers are moving their content online and working to find successful and sustainable online business models. Managers of centralised information repositories are exploring a number of funding models. Resources such as PubMed and ERIC are substantially funded through government sources. Many resources are being made freely available online and being funded through advertising revenue. Taking a somewhat different approach, Wikipedia is a non-profit corporation receiving its funding from donations. Major funders including Dell Computing and the Virgin Foundation have contributed financially to Wikipedia. Google has recently announced that they are working on a free encyclopaedia funded by advertising that they are calling "*Knol*". Many other resources are funded by paid membership, or like the *Encyclopaedia Britannica,* they offer some combination of freely available material and materials paid for by subscription.

The evolution of Open WorldCat is demonstrating the possibilities for Internet-wide library services. But it is also an illustration of the difficulties to be overcome as library processes evolve. With the coming of Open WorldCat, libraries are placing a whole new emphasis on keeping individual library's shared holdings information up to date. OCLC WorldCat is a library cataloguing repository of long standing. It is important both as a source of shared cataloguing records and as a library holdings union catalogue for inter-library lending. Until recently there has not been an overriding emphasis put on keeping library holdings information in WorldCat up to date. Libraries commonly submitted cataloguing records to OCLC, but many libraries did not submit information about deletions from their catalogues or changes to serials holdings. One of the primary uses of the database was as a source of MARC records. MARC records provided by a particular library continued to be useful to other libraries seeking copy even if that material was no longer held by the originating library. It was also not uncommon for libraries to discontinue reporting to OCLC for periods of time. There is a substantial cost to libraries and OCLC to check and update the content of World Cat to ensure that it accurately reflects their current holdings. The 1980s and 1990s were a time of great change in library serials collections in particular. The serials price crunch and then the advent of leased online journals have meant that many libraries have been consistently cutting paper serials collections and more recently adding large numbers of online titles. Open WorldCat has become a public resource for locating library materials and for accurately and seamlessly linking web search results to local libraries where particular materials can be borrowed. OCLC and its partner libraries have had to pay new attention to getting and keeping the holdings information in Open WorldCat up to date. The next step would seem to be to develop automated and interactive methods of exchanging holding information between library catalogues and OCLC.

11

Library application services for information exchange: more and less than web services

The notion that different applications and repositories can act as service providers to other applications is well established in Internet computing. More simply, the World Wide Web makes it possible to pass a URL-like string of characters over the Internet from one application to another; requesting the return of a particular webpage or document; a particular piece of information, or requesting that the application perform a particular action, such as a search. The ability to request services by passing information in an HTML formatted URL string is fundamental to how the World Wide Web works.

The networked information environment relies on several important methods for linking applications together and passing information between applications. Many web applications use informal methods to link online services together in an array of mashups (see Chapter 12: Mashups). More formal standards are emerging to provide for robust and uniform exchange of information between online systems. The emerging model of distributed library resources is built on both formal and informal methods.

The OpenURL standard for locating and requesting

information resources underlies link resolver technology and much of the linking between ILSs and other resources. The OpenURL standard is described as follows:

> The OpenURL Framework Standard defines architecture for creating OpenURL Framework Applications. An OpenURL Framework Application is a networked service environment, in which packages of information are transported over a network. These packages have a description of a referenced resource at their core, and they are transported with the intent of obtaining context-sensitive services pertaining to the referenced resource. To enable the recipients of these packages to deliver such context-sensitive services, each package describes the referenced resource itself, the network context in which the resource is referenced, and the context in which the service request takes place.

> The Standard specifies how to construct these packages as representations of abstract information constructs called ContextObjects. To this end, the OpenURL Framework Standard defines the following core components: Character Encoding, Serialization, Constraint Language, ContextObject Format, Metadata Format, and Namespace. (NISO, 2005)

The OpenURL standard is formalising the methods used to send and receive information between different systems in URL strings. The integration of library systems will be greatly enhanced when every content database, repository and search interface offers services using this standard.

APIs are gateways into networked software applications that allow other software applications to ask them for information or send them instructions. APIs are common with many large applications including ILS and federated search software. APIs were developed so that customised programs would be written that interact with library systems in new ways. APIs provide a means of interacting with software that will be stable over a long period of time, regardless of any changes that take place to the software. APIs are an important step forward over informal methods of interacting with online software, such as screen scraping, which may need to be changed any time an application changes the way it displays or presents information. As an example, the State University of California customised library search interface, Xerxes, was developed using Muse Global federated search software's X-Server API tools. Many libraries have found APIs complex and time consuming to use in application development. Typically these interfaces require programming in a high level language. Many libraries do not have the in-house technical expertise or the programmer time to devote to developing custom applications using APIs. Like so many library application features, until libraries use them extensively, APIs will not be fully developed by the vendor companies.

Recently, web companies such as Google and Amazon have developed lightweight, highly simplified API-like tools for working with their applications. Their APIs have proven relatively easy to learn and fast to develop useful applications with. They have proven very popular, so they have placed pressure for the APIs of online vendor systems to become ever simpler and easier to use. A growing number of e-commerce sites on the World Wide Web are offering a range of web service APIs. These services are often developed to use online interchange protocols such as Simple Object Access Protocol (SOAP), and the even simpler Representational State Transfer (REST) (Udell, 2005). Such web services can be used to provide

Figure 11.1 URLs for web services

URL call to Syndetics Solutions Inc. for a book over image for a particular ISBN number

http://www.syndetics.com/index.aspx?type=xw12&isbn=0553477722/SC.GIF&client=???

Any ISBN number

Paid service, Client ID required.

A basic URL call to Amazon requesting a book cover image for a particular ISBN number

http://images.amazon.com/images/P/0770428495.01.TZZZZZZZ.jpg (A thumbnail image.)

http://images.amazon.com/images/P/0195122623.01.LZZZZZZZ.jpg (Large format image.)

A URL call to Google Images, displays the same book cover image via the Indigo book store

http://google.com/images?q=tbn:IDLifgH6HhbcoM:http://dynamic.images.indigo

URL call to the xISBN service for ISBN's related to a particular ISBN

http://xisbn.worldcat.org/webservices/xid/isbn/0771008805

A URL search of Google Images for book cover images by ISBN.

http://images.google.com/images?hl=en&q=0770428495

information using straightforward HTML instructions. Hopefully, the trend will continue towards simpler, more standardised methods for exchanging information between systems, which are easily accessible to all libraries.

It is common to speak of using library applications such as link resolvers, or search applications, as services that provide information to other applications. Any online application to which you can send a request over the Internet and receive a response can be seen as a basic web service. True web services are more tightly defined and standardised processes. Nonetheless, a great deal of integration customisation is not done using formal APIs or true web services but is done using simple HTML or underlying computer exchange standards such as SQL and ODBC (Figure 11.1).

Tools such as link resolvers, federated search applications and library catalogues can be used as sources of services, instead of seeing them simply as stand alone applications with a single interface. It is more useful to see them as service tools that can be accessed in many ways, from many locations on the web, using many different interfaces.

This changes how we view the library ILS. Instead of being a repository accessed by a single user interface, it can be seen as a service engine that delivers a variety of metadata services in a standardised way to any application that needs them, from a specific search interface to a toolbar lookup application or a web browser library lookup. The metadata that is stored in library repositories must be determined by the needs of the applications using those repositories as services. As lookup applications struggle with multiple ISBN numbers, or inaccurate e-journal routing URLs, it seems that some of the needed metadata is not yet readily available from library repository services.

Library lookup tools such as Umlaut use the library catalogue as a service to check for library holdings whenever a searcher encounters material in their web searching that might be available from their local libraries. Web browser plugins such as LibX or Book Burro also use the library catalogue as a kind of service to check for availability of materials found in web searches. In the same way, Google and other search engines, as well as OCLC Open WorldCat, have all established relationships with the library link resolving companies and ILS vendors, so that when a web searcher locates a reference in search results he or she can be routed to their local link resolver or local library to determine if full text is available.

Library online search resources are increasingly being used as search services that simply respond to information requests from other services. Subject specific searches can be tailored to particular groups of users, and offered from course information systems such as Web CT and Blackboard. In the university environment, it is possible to use federated search software to create hundreds of customised subject specific search services. A subject specialised search box can be placed on the webpage of each academic discipline, department, or each individual course. The Joint Information Systems Committee (JISC) in the UK has funded a number of projects aimed at using library resources to provide content services to virtual learning environments. This work has included providing personalised library content services to courseware users (JISC, 2007).

Most large collections of e-journal content cover many subjects. The databases of large publishers, as well as aggregator databases, are internally subject divided. It is possible to create individual search targets for each subject division in each database. Subject focused searching is one of the advantages of specialised databases. The ability to remove extraneous material from your search at the outset is a major benefit of these databases. Lack of subject focus has been one of the disadvantages of federated search tools. This lack of subject focus is also growing problem with Internet searching as the volume of material increases. The ability to customised federated searches that target subject subdivided portions of different databases is a very powerful new tool. Federated search applications are being used to offer a wide range of customised search combinations to meet many specialised needs.

The major web browser companies have built custom search features into the Microsoft Internet Explorer browser and the Mozilla Firefox browser. Many libraries make library catalogue searches available from the search browser. The major web browsers, Microsoft Internet

Explorer and Firefox, support the Open Search format. Open Search is a popular format developed by Amazon that allows searches to be sent to many web search applications. Open Search is primarily intended to search freely available public web resources. However, when using the Open Search format, it is relatively easy to offer library users authenticated search services to many major databases and federated search applications from the search features built into web browsers or from customised web pages (Webster, 2007a) (Figures 11.2 and 11.3).

Figure 11.2 **Passing search requests via URL**

Basic Search.

http://www3.interscience.wiley.com/search/allsearch?mode=quicksearch&WISindexid1= WISall&WISsearch1=trees

Keywords to be searched

Subject search targeting only Physics and Astronomy.

http://www3.interscience.wiley.com/search/allsearch?&subjects=PHYS&mode =quicksearch&WISindexid1=WISall&WISsearch1=tree

SpringerLink URL search request, targeting the humanites-social sciences-law section of SpringerLink.

http://www.springerlink.com/humanities-social-sciences-and-law/ ?sortorder=asc&mode=allwords&k={tree}

Muse Global federated search URL string, targeting a General purpose selection of databases.

http://LocalMuseServer.edu:8000/muse/servlet/MusePeer?action=logon&userID= XXXFoundation&userPWD=&dbList=GENERAL&templateFile=passThrough.html&query=tree

Paid service with ID unique to each library

While libraries use a variety of methods to build services with their online resources, more formalised web services are being developed to allow library resources to interact in simpler, more consistent ways. A well-known IBM description of web services states that:

Figure 11.3   **Search request URL used in toolbars and inserted in webpages**

```
<?xml version="1.0" encoding="UTF-8" ?>
<OpenSearchDescription xmlns="xmlns="http://a9.com/-/spec/opensearch/1.1/"
xmlns:moz="http://www.mozilla.org/2006/browser/search/">
<ShortName>google</ShortName>
<ShortName>Springer-LINK</ShortName>
<Description>Covers journals in the following subject areas: life sciences, chemical sciences,
geosciences, computer sciences, mathematics, medicine, physics &amp; astronomy, engineering,
environmental sciences, law, and economics.</Description>
<InputEncoding>UTF-8</InputEncoding>
<Url type="text/html" method="GET" template="http://LocalEasyProxy:2048/login?url=http://
www.springerlink.com/content/?k={searchTerms}"></Url>
<moz:SearchForm>http://LocalEasyProxy:2048/login?url=http://www.springerlink.com/</
moz:SearchForm>
</OpenSearchDescription>       Proxy prepend for local
                               library Ezproxy server
```

A Muse Global Search with html form tags to creat a webpage search box on any webpage.

```
<form name="quickSearch" id="quickSearch" method="get" action="http:///LocalMuseServer.edu:8000/
muse/servlet/MusePeer"
target="_blank">
    Article Quick Search
     <input name="action" value="logon" type="hidden" />
     <input name="userID" value="XXXFoundation" type="hidden" />
     <input name="userPwd" value="" type="hidden" />
     <input name="dbList" value="GENERAL" type="hidden" />
     <input name="templateFile" value="passThrough.html" type="hidden" />
     <input name="query" type="text" size="50" />
     <input type="submit" name="Submit" value="Search" />
    </form>
```

Web services are a technology that allows applications to communicate with each other in a platform- and programming language-independent manner. A web service is a software interface that describes a collection of operations that can be accessed over the network through standardized XML messaging. It uses protocols based on the XML language to describe an operation to execute or data to exchange with another web service. A group of web services interacting together in this manner defines a particular web service application in a service-oriented architecture (SOA).

The software industry is finally coming to terms with the fact that integrating software applications across multiple operating systems, programming languages and hardware platforms is not something that can be solved by any one particular proprietary environment. Traditionally, the problem has been one of tight-coupling, where one application that calls a remote network is tied strongly to it by the function call it makes and the parameters it requests. In most systems before web services, this is a fixed interface with little flexibility or adaptability to changing environments or needs.

Web services use XML that can describe any and all data in a truly platform-independent manner for exchange across systems, thus moving towards loosely-coupled applications. Furthermore, web services can function on a more abstract level that can re-evaluate, modify or handle data types dynamically on demand. So, on a technical level, web services can handle data much easier and allow software to communicate more freely.

On a higher conceptual level, we can look at web services as units of work, each handling a specific functional task. One step above this, the tasks can be combined into business-oriented tasks to handle particular business operational tasks, and this in turn allows non-technical people to think of applications that can handle business issues together in a workflow of web services applications. Thus, once the web services are designed and built by technical people, business process architects can aggregate them into solving business level problems. To borrow a car engine analogy, a business process architect can think of putting together a whole car engine with the car frame, body, transmission and other systems, rather than look at the many pieces within each engine. Furthermore, the dynamic platform means that the engine can work together with the transmission or parts from other car manufacturers.

What rises from this last aspect is that web services are helping to bridge the gap between business people and technologists in an organization. Web services make it easier for business people to understand technical operations. Business people can describe events and activities and technologists can associate them with appropriate services.

With universally defined interfaces and well-designed tasks, it also becomes easier to reuse these tasks and thus, the applications they represent. Reusability of application software means a better return on investment on software because it can produce more from the same resources. It allows business people to consider using an existing application in a new way or offering it to a partner in a new way, thus potentially increasing the business transactions between partners.

Therefore, the primary issues that web services tries to tackle are the issues of data and application integration, and that of transforming technical functions into business-oriented computing tasks. These two facets allow businesses to communicate on a process or application level with their partners, while leaving dynamic room to adapt to new situations or work with different partners on demand. (IBM, 2007)

The web services for library applications may prove to be a

simpler alternative to proprietary APIs for exchanging information. A web service should epitomise the notion of modularity. You send a web service a simple request and it returns an answer. The OCLC xISBN service is a case in point. This service was created to help libraries identify multiple ISSN numbers that refer to different editions or formats of the same book. You send it an ISBN number and it searches WorldCat to return all related ISBN numbers. So if a searcher finds an interesting audio book on the web and wishes to know if their library has the book, the xISBN service provides a means for seeking ISBN numbers of all hard cover, soft cover, audio or e-book editions of the work. (OCLC WorldCat, undated).

Library applications developers are employing web services to allow the functionality of their resources to be easily accessed by other applications. A large number of standardised web services can be developed for many of the key search, linking and retrieval functions performed by library resources. Library service and content vendors are actively developing web services. Recognising the need to work cooperatively, a group was formed called the Vendor Initiative for Enabling Web Services (VIEWS), which was described as follows:

> VIEWS is an initiative by vendors and library service organizations launched in June 2004 aimed at the enabling of web services between disparate applications used in libraries. Chaired by Carl Grant, President & CEO of VTLS, this initiative is a response to the growing need in the vendor and library service communities to create both a discussion forum and a plan to implement web services. The group that has agreed to cooperate in the initiative includes: Dynix, Fretwell Downing, Index Data, Muse Global, OCLC,

Endeavor, Talis and VTLS. NISO has been invited to monitor this work and keep the NISO membership informed of developments and emerging opportunities for formal standardization activities. (NISO Views Initiative, 2007)

The VIEWS initiative describes web services in the following terms:

Web services is the next dimension in systems architecture. It builds on core standards including at the foundation: TCP/IP, HTTP and XML. Using new technologies, the core of web services will be the ability for software to interoperate at many different levels, thus resulting in a more seamless integration of functional capabilities for end users of the products. The technology is already seeing rapid adoption in the traditional business sectors, with companies like Amazon, Home Depot, Google and others building business processes using the technology. In the library marketplace, many vendors are already offering applications that support web service, including Dynix, Index Data and VTLS. To reach the ultimate goal of web services, true interoperability, the vendors will need to work out guidelines and possibly standards, which will extend the foundation. (VTLS, 2004)

This work resulted in the release of "Best practices for designing web services in the library context", by the NISO Web Services and Practices working group. This report begins by saying:

Purpose and scope – This effort outlines the actual and potential uses of web services in a library context. As the nature of web services is changing rapidly, this is only a snapshot in time. The intent is to be helpful, not limiting. Web services are seen as an alternative to fully developed application programming interfaces (API) for circumstances in which the additional overhead is not warranted. Many works exist to explain technical features of web service interactions. The intended audiences are people from both the vendor and user community who seek to understand the role and potential of web services in aspects of library work. (NISO Web Services and Practices Working Group, 2006a)

However, having drafted a best practices document this web services working group then suspended its work with the following comment:

The NISO Web Services and Practices Working Group, after spending several months on its charge to create a best practices document, has concluded that the time is not right for this group to complete this task. The current web services landscape is still in development and the group feels it is too early to write such a "backwards-facing" document. Members of this group came together, largely drawn from the then-inactive VIEWS group, expecting various things, from a VIEWS-like survey of problem areas needing standards to a narrow focus on a particular area of difficulty to a state-of-the-universe overview. The group feels that there are problems in the library/web services interface that need to be tackled with standards efforts, such as system frameworks and architecture (particularly around connecting) and an e-framework in the e-learning area. There is strong consensus that NISO would benefit in some areas from working with existing efforts (such as the UK-based e-learning efforts) and in some cases in using its vantage point in the standards world to identify areas in which a broader set of standards, perhaps starting as an extension of existing standards, might bring wider usage and constituency .

This group leaves its white paper on web services as its deliverable, and recommends that NISO sponsor work in the e-learning environment and/or in the connection infrastructure area (such as how to discover existing services and how to connect services to servers and to each other). (NISO Web Services and Practices Working Group, 2006b)

Web services are likely to have a central role in connecting different library resources together and making library content easily accessible from many locations. Although the potential to profoundly change automated library services is clear, further developments in library web services are still to come.

The Open Archives Initiative's Protocol for Metadata Harvesting (OAI-PMH) may well prove to be one of the most important service standards for libraries. OAI-PMH is described as follows:

The Open Archives Initiative's Protocol for Metadata Harvesting (OAI-PMH) was created to facilitate discovery of distributed resources. The OAI-PMH achieves this by providing a simple, yet powerful framework for metadata harvesting. Harvesters can incrementally gather records contained in OAI-PMH repositories and use them to create services covering the content of several repositories. The OAI-PMH has been widely accepted, and until recently, it has mainly been applied to make Dublin Core metadata about scholarly objects contained in distributed repositories searchable through a single user interface. (Van de Sompel, 2003)

This interchange standard provides means for any metadata repository, including ILSs, to be made available for automated indexing by network indexing services. It is commonly used to exchange and aggregate indexing information from many large web-based repositories, including local institutional repositories. Relatively few libraries are using it yet to expose their library catalogues to automated harvesting.

More elements of the integrated information environment

12.1 Object oriented principles, relational structure and modularity

Relational database software and concepts are a basic part of library systems. Virtually all databases used in libraries including ILSs and e-content databases work with a relational structure whereby information stored in one database table can be accessed in a seamless way by other tables. A number of standards such as SQL and ODBC exist to allow database information to be exchanged not only between different tables in a relational structure but also between remote and disparate database systems. The integration between Windows Access databases and Excel spreadsheets is fundamental to materials management in libraries, as it is in most other management environments. Within the computer software industry efforts at integrating the movement of data between software applications are very longstanding.

Many of today's computer applications use a variety of standards and approaches in an effort to be highly modular, with each application exchanging information freely with other applications. Older computer programming methods required each component of a program or larger system to be customised to work with other parts of the program or system. Each piece of the software system was dependent on the others. Any change to such software often required rewriting all of the related components. Computer programming has largely moved away from these methods, and is now based on object oriented principles, described as follows:

> Object-oriented programming is a methodology for creating programs using collections of self-sufficient objects that have encapsulated data and behavior and that act upon, request, and interact with each other by passing messages back and forth. (Winblad et al., 1990)

Modern computer programs are written in pieces. Each segment is designed to receive set inputs in a standardised way, and produce standardised output. Programs are written with the understanding that the activities the program must perform will change over time, but that the existing components can be reused in new ways. A software component may receive input from different sources and its output may be processed differently, but that segment of programming continues to be useful. Large programs such as operating systems (e.g. Windows) must be written in a way that allows them to be adapted and changed in a very flexible manner over a long period of time.

Today's library systems share a number of parallels with computer programs. Libraries developed monolithic propriety systems with only a few carefully customised linkages between systems. Our library catalogues have grown to include very large numbers of URL links to e-content and additional metadata. Like large computer programs, they are becoming increasingly unwieldy and difficult, if not impossible, to maintain.

The distributed information management environment continues to develop as a modular environment where different components perform unique functions and share their work with other components through web services and standardised data interchange. Without delving too deeply into the complex area of object-oriented design, we have an opportunity to look to some basic object oriented principles to develop powerful new library systems.

12.2 Open source

Open source software is already playing a major role in the emergence of a more integrated, distributed information environment. A large number of libraries use common open source software. The Linux server operating system, Apache web servers, MySQL database software and the Firefox web browser are just a few examples.

Open source applications offer a low cost means for libraries with limited resources to have access to important new software tools. A growing number of libraries will otherwise be unable to bear the extra costs associated with online systems such as link resolving, federated searching, or enhanced search interfaces.

Of course, the quality and reliability of open source software varies a great deal. Deploying, configuring and maintaining open source software has often required a commitment in time and technological skills, which puts it beyond the facilities of many libraries. But open source applications are becoming more reliable, fully developed, and much easier to deploy and maintain. Firefox or the Open Office software suite are downloaded and used by many thousands of users with no special instructions.

Open source library applications, such as the Evergreen

and Koha ILSs, the course management system Moodle, the ReSearcher suite of library linking and integration tools or the IndexData company's Zebra indexing engine are providing viable alternatives to vendor applications for library integration. As open source software becomes more accessible, and under-resourced libraries can deploy these applications at low cost and with limited technical expertise, open source applications may in the near future have a revolutionary role to play. Marshall Breeding recently noted that:

> Conditions are ripe for a more rapid adoption of one source ILS than we have seen in the past. There are at least three viable products and options available for commercial support. The concept of open source software has become very popular in our field; many librarians are discouraged with the commercial ILS vendors. I frequently hear complaints about the low level of innovation and the high cost of automation software. The success of a large consortium and the few mid-size libraries with open source ILSs provides a strong dose of reassurance to others that this approach can work. These events have primed the pump: we'll have to wait and see how strong the stream of adoption flows over the next few years. (Breeding, 2007)

Perhaps even more important than the lower cost of open source systems is the fact that they have provided the tools for libraries to innovate, experiment and customise methods of integrating their services, without depending on software vendors. The open source web browser Firefox is perhaps one of the best examples of an open source application that has fostered large amounts of innovation and a wealth of new services. Open systems can be fully open source products with unrestricted licences, and full rights for anyone to access and modify the source computer code. But they can also simply be systems designed to be easily modified and to easily interact with other systems. Amazon's web services are an example of an open, but not open source, resource that has succeeded in fostering great amounts of innovation, while providing standards that unify technological innovation.

In some important areas of applications development, libraries doing their own customised development are ahead of software vendors. LibX and XC are good examples of this. They are developing products with integration features that cannot be purchased commercially. As open source applications become more sophisticated and accessible they also put very healthy pressure on commercial application vendors to provide innovative customer focused services, while working to moderate their pricing. Libraries will continue to debate the benefits of open source vs. vendor provided applications in their individual circumstances, but there is no question that open source development had a major effect in moving the integration of the information environment forward.

12.3 Standards

An article by Betty Landesmann and Beth Weston has the lovely title "Barbarism is the absence of standards: applying standards to untangle the electronic jumble" (Landesmann and Weston, 1999). Information standards will be at the very centre of libraries' efforts to integrate their resources and the online information environment as a whole. Standardisation is essential in the movement toward universal discovery and access. There are a number of new and developing standards aimed at fostering better integration of online information services. The current focus on tying e-content resources together is demonstrated by a look at the list of current working groups of the National Information Standards Organization (NISO) in the USA. These include:

- The License Expression Working Group to develop a single standard for the exchange of licence information between publishers and libraries.

- The ONIX for Serials NISO/EDItEUR Joint Working Party, looking into the automated exchange of descriptive metadata for serials.

- A three-part metasearch initiative to standardize federated searching, with separate task groups on access management, collection description and search/retrieval.

- The Standardized Usage Statistics Harvesting Initiative (SUSHI), to develop a standard for the automated exchange of electronic content database use statistics.

- NISO/ALPSP Working Group on Versions of Journal Articles to develop processes for distinguishing between different electronic versions of journals.

(NISO, 2007)

From a materials management perspective it is noteworthy that this work deals with standardised metadata, but very little of it is metadata that can be managed in traditional ILSs. It is also important to note that the focus of this standards work is on developing automated means, whereby metadata is exchanged between management systems without human intervention.

A major effort to establish standards for online resources has gone on over the last decade, beginning with Z39.50. But standards on their own are not proving to be a single solution to the challenges of integration. In many cases, progress is being made by turning away from existing standards. Within the standards community, there has been discussion about why standards such as NCIP have not received wider acceptance and deployment. Z39.50 has had the widest acceptance in the library community. But it has become the standard for sharing library catalogue searches only. Z39.50 has not penetrated into other search areas outside the library community. There is a progressive movement from complex to simpler, increasingly lightweight standards. When standards are overly complex, vendors and custom developers may deploy them only partially. Application developers may forgo the standards in favour of faster and easier approaches. Older, more complex standards are being superseded by simpler standards.

There is a dynamic tension between standards and innovation. An overly rigid adherence to standards can stifle innovation. Innovation often takes place by going beyond, and defying, existing standards. Innovators compete to have their latest approach become the new standard. Often there is a competitive race to set an informal standard, and then seek to have that standard formalised. As often as not, this is simply an effort by one company to corner the market for its technology. We have seen standards battles in a number of popular media, including video recording, high definition television and computer operating systems. This process of innovation is important to development of better tools and services, but it is chaotic and leaves libraries wondering which way to jump, which materials formats to adopt, and which standards to follow. As is often the case in libraries today, it leaves us making customised and ad hoc innovations to our systems while we wait for better standardised methods.

Of course, standards are highly subject to interpretation in their implementation. Typically, successful standards have required long and difficult processes of definition, before they work effectively and consistently across many different vendor implementations, and therefore provide the greatest integration benefits. This was the case with Z39.50. It is also the case with NCIP.

Standards must be subject to change. The Z39.50 standard is being extended by XML-based search standards. The improvement of processes and the evolution of their standards must be ongoing. There are a number of cases where the formal or informal standards we are currently using are well known to be flawed and in need of replacement by something better, but they will continue to be used until better approaches come along.

A number of the processes that libraries currently rely on are expedients only. IP number authentication for access to licensed materials is a good example. IP validation has a number of security and practical shortcomings. Online content vendors have been seeking alternatives for some time. Very popular proxy server technology is built on working around IP authentication and redirecting IP number traffic. A proxy server takes each proxied transaction and redirects it, acting as a trusted intermediary between a user PC and a licensed e-content provider. Therefore the use of proxy servers unnecessarily increases network traffic, often more than doubling the traffic of the online transactions being proxied. This slows down online transactions passing through a proxy server and reduces the reliability of these transactions. A replacement for IP methods of authentication and proxy service is needed. There are several alternative systems whereby e-content vendors and libraries join in highly secure and trusted networks, and content vendors can receive authentication for any client PC requesting service without having to rely on IP validation. But IP validation and proxy servers will remain until alternatives become widely available and used.

Standards are a critical tool, but it is up to libraries to clearly understand the potential of these tools. Their full benefits are realised only when libraries are willing to use and fully deploy them and prevail upon software vendors to fully and consistently implement standards.

12.4 Mashups

In the last couple of years web mashups have become common and popular. These are network applications that bring together elements from several different applications to create new functionality. Mashups have been defined as follows:

> This merging of services and content from multiple web sites in an integrated, coherent way is called a "mashup". Most mashups do more than simply integrate services and content. Sites that do mashups typically add value. They benefit users in a way that's different and better than the individual services they leverage. It suggests that though there can be different definitions of mashups. "If a web site uses

data or functionality from another web site and combines it in an application, it's a mashup". (Ort et al., 2007)

PC Magazine's Encyclopedia defines mashup as:

A mixture of content or elements. For example, an application that was built from routines from multiple sources or a web site that combines content and/or scripts from multiple sources is said to be a mashup. (PCMag.com Encyclopedia, undated).

Mashups have been an item of considerable interest in the library community. Many of the informal methods libraries are using to customise search access to databases, or locate citation information from web sources, or make connections from library catalogues to online bookstores, or authenticating users via proxy servers, can be described as mashups. Library applications were often created with relatively narrow methods of use in mind. Libraries have found ways to use these applications in broader ways, link them with other services to create richer, more integrated service experiences for particular users.

Systems librarians currently live in a world where the only barriers are our imaginations and the available time. There was a time when conversations at library IT conferences often turned to "why can't you", search your library OPAC and web search engines at the same time, or put XML formatted records into your OPAC, or store all MARC data in a single worldwide repository. Today, we operate with the understanding that anything is possible. With the programming tools available, the basic openness of html and the World Wide Web environment and the level of interoperability that we have achieved so far, mean that any form of integration is technically possible, with sufficient time and effort. This is an exciting place to be.

Libraries have become very adept at finding formal and informal ways to link their systems together. They are building custom search interfaces and portals, which pull information from dozens of sources to present that information to users. The framework of a distributed information environment is in place in many librarians. The integrated environment that is emerging allows for the exchange of information between federated search interfaces, library ILSs, link resolvers, and between these library systems and publishers, vendors and agents, as well as centralised resources such as the Library of Congress, OCLC and Crossref.

Integration of both library user interfaces and management systems means more than tying only library systems together. Library systems connect with university and college campus systems. They can provide services to state or regional government information systems and share information with online tourism resources, museums and other cultural institutions. There are large opportunities to make appropriate connections and exchange data with other information systems.

Library ILSs routinely have standardised methods for exchanging secure patron information with other systems. Most common is industry standard LDAP, which is used for interacting with student ID computer systems. Technically it is a relatively straightforward matter for library systems to exchange information about library card holders or to rely on some other system such as a campus ID system, or even a state driver's licence system for patron metadata.

The current information environment provides libraries

with an array of integration tools. These include Z39.50, several XML-based search protocols, the highly customisable features of HTML and related webpage technologies and the underlying hyperlinking principles of the World Wide Web. The standards of the computer industry such as LDAP, ODBC and SQL also form part of the available tool set. We can add to this a growing number of web services for online applications.

Elements of the new distributed model are all around us. However in the library world too many of these tools are only partially developed. An example is the number of e-content database products that still lack a freely available standards-based federated search interface. When integration tools are available, they are often complex, difficult to use, and indifferently supported by applications vendors. The concept of a mashup often connotes custom made or cobbled together. Too often integration of library systems is still a matter of customising connections between systems. The model for a distributed information environment is becoming clear, even before some of the necessary systems and features are fully in place to implement this model.

Yet, when I speak to vendor representatives, they express surprise that there are concerns about proprietary and siloed systems with limited or cumbersome tools for interacting with other systems. Library applications vendor have been developing a variety of tools for integrating their products into the larger network, and some are beginning to fully understand the new online environment. Integration is still seen as a matter of interest to a few libraries with the resources and expertise to customise, rather than a core feature of library systems available to every library. Library developers seem to be well ahead of system vendors in understanding the new information environment. Yet few librarians are raising questions about integration features with vendors. All too often, I am told, "no one has ever asked for that before".

13

Conclusions

Electronic materials are an enormous resource that has transformed the services libraries can offer their users. But they present a fragmented and often confusing array of materials to information seekers. From many different quarters, the library industry is coming to consensus on a number of issues concerning these resources. The problems of integrating electronic materials are being pursued from many different directions, from library cataloguing to user interface development, to standards development.

Simply providing reliable means for existing systems to be linked together is not an end in itself. In the short term, libraries, content and applications vendors are developing methods for linking online resources together and maintaining information about their interconnections. In the longer term our efforts should be focused on simpler, more standardised and more globally uniform methods of integration. The end libraries are pursuing is a more unified information environment, where virtually all materials can be easily searched, and where searchers can then seamlessly access all content that is readily available to them. This goal will involve developing very different systems where global information repositories are searched along with local repositories. A few search interfaces will discover information from a wide selection of different sources. Context appropriate searches will be available from a host of different online locations.

Our early approaches to integration and achieving a more unified information environment have revolved around putting additional information about electronic materials into library catalogues. This has been a valuable and successful effort.

Nonetheless, there is growing agreement that centralised catalogue information in many individual monolithic library catalogues is not a sustainable approach. It is an approach that has resulted in an inefficient duplication of effort, as many agencies store and maintain the same information. As libraries store ever-larger amounts of rapidly changing metadata, limited staffing and overly labour dependent methods place limits on how far libraries can take the centralised strategy. Libraries are increasingly reviewing their processes and make realistic determinations of their long-term sustainability and seeking new ways to reduce duplication of effort. More efficient, automated methods are needed to keep up with the growing volume of electronic materials and the rate at which they change.

13.1 Distributed and shared access and materials management

To access and manage the large array of electronic resources, libraries have come to rely on a distributed set of repositories rather that on the single library ILS. Libraries and electronic content vendors have a common need for the same metadata. Metadata is often duplicated by individual libraries and vendors and sometimes even duplicated multiple times by the same library. It has been clear for some time that libraries cannot succeed in locally maintaining all metadata they need for today's information access using current methods of cataloguing. Libraries and content vendors alike must move from seeing their role as the sole keepers of independent metadata repositories, to seeing their role as partners in maintaining metadata in multiple shared and distributed repositories. Shared information management will be an important element in ensuring the long-term sustainability of library management practices. Libraries and the e-content industry will continue to build on their partnerships to share the workload of maintaining accurate and up-to-date information about e-serials, e-books and other e-materials. Finding the right mix between efficiency, cost effectiveness, accuracy, reliability and timeliness will continue to be a challenge in these partnerships.

13.2 New search combinations and points of user access

Federated search technology has been developed to integrate access to the wide selection of online resources libraries now offer. Library users are best served by being able to search multiple information repositories and e-content sources together. The federated search tools available can be used to offer users innumerable different search interfaces that meet their needs in different online locations, situations and contexts. The local library catalogue, regional library catalogues, on demand document delivery services and other inter-library lending servers can be searched together, as an extension of the library OPAC search and represented as common results for users.

Libraries are taking on the role of providing search services from many online locations and interfaces where library users may need information. User interfaces include subject specific searches, on course information web pages, theme or purpose specific web pages. They also include searches from web browser tool bars and automatic library lookup searches, which may link users to available library content without them specifically asking for it. Electronic content materials can be searched in a great number of subject grouping, theme groupings, or selections by material type. Federated searches allows us to completely rethink the idea of an OPAC or primary library search, as well as the many other search combinations library offer their users.

13.3 Seamlessness

Libraries have developed linking technologies to make connections between search results and available full-text e-content. The next logical step in the process of integrating fragmented online information is to go beyond linking to simplify search and retrieval processes. An important new role for libraries is to make the users path from resource selection, to search, to full-text retrieval, as effortless as possible. The growing emphasis on a seamless user transaction places new demands on our materials management systems. These systems must be able to easily expose needed metadata in a variety of new ways as part of many search and access processes. Library management systems must be able to provide the accurate and entirely up-to-date metadata needed to drive user search and retrieval processes.

13.4 Silo busting

Although we have begun to tie diverse online sources together, silo busting remains a key role for libraries. Making connections between data repositories and linking resources through standardised interchange methods and common data formats are at part of efforts to break open proprietary information silos. But it is also critical to continue reducing the number of online interfaces and individual information repositories whenever possible. The fewer interfaces users must deal with the better. One single online repository may not be achievable, or even desirable. Specialised databases are important. There will always be a place for Medline and PsychInfo. But there is no reason they should not be searched with the same interface or searchable with any number of interfaces of the users' choosing.

Our efforts at integrating online information include working to separate content from search and retrieval interfaces, and deal with the issues associated with each separately. The fact that there are too many search interfaces continues to be one of the most obvious problems with our environment. Libraries should be considering questions of interoperability with each search interface they ask library users to tolerate. It is important to consider if there are alternatives to bringing one more into the world? It is important to discuss with content vendors how search interfaces seeking like content can be merged or made interoperable.

13.5 Taking information management to the network level

We are seeing more and more opportunities to go beyond the shared and distributed management of online materials to develop centralised, global repositories and services to provide online materials management information.

The shared approach to information management leads easily to new systems where essential management information is collected centrally, at the global level, so it can be used as needed by local information facilitators (the local libraries). We have the ability to develop shared open and centralised repositories where essential metadata such as serials package journal title lists, or persistent URLs to e-content are stored once only and accessed multiple times by all systems. Libraries should be actively working toward such centralised solutions, while resisting the view that metadata is a proprietary priced commodity. Online information managers have worked to reduce unnecessary duplication of metadata. They have worked to aggregate metadata in as few places as practical, and to aggregate metadata as close to the creator of the content as possible.

Global information management repositories and services are a natural extension of this effort.

13.6 The unified and integrated online information environment

Libraries' efforts to unify and integrate online information will involve maintaining a balance between competing forces. Efforts to centralise information in library catalogues have strict limitations. But the decentralised approach involving multiple repositories and broadcast searches to innumerable individual e-content repositories also has major shortcomings. In the interests of better integration libraries are current building ever more complex systems, which are dependent on a greater and greater number of linkages and interactions between systems. In the long run, such systems must become unwieldy, and only marginally less so if standardised methods of information exchange are used. The complexity of integrating relationships between our systems must have limits.

But the Google approach also has its shortcomings. Today's generalised web search is a very crude tool, compared to the subject focused and feature rich search capabilities of specialised e-content databases. Libraries' efforts at creating global metadata repositories and centralised search standards are in early stages of development and deployment. Each of these approaches to unifying electronic material has been successful to some extent. Libraries are successfully using a number of applications and approaches for integrating access to the resources they make available. But they have not yet solved the problems of the disintegrated information environment.

Better integration of the information environment will come from the use of various approaches in different situations and a series of compromises between centralising metadata locally, sharing metadata in global repositories and using different methods to search multiple repositories. As yet there is no clear answer to how the balance between local and global, or between centralised and decentralised repositories will be worked out. Libraries will continue to use all available means to make online materials more easily accessible to their users. A new model of materials management is emerging. The tools currently at our disposal make it possible to build a more powerful universal information resource than we have now.

References

Antelman, K., Lynema, E. and Pace, A.K. (2006) 'Toward a twenty-first century library catalog', *Information Technology and Libraries,* September: 128–39.

Apps, A. (2004) 'The OpenURL and OpenURL framework: demystifying link resolution', *Ariadne,* 38: available at *http://www.ariadne.ac.uk/issue38/apps-rpt/.*

Apps, A. and MacIntyre, R. (2006) 'Why OpenURL?', *D-Lib Magazine,* 12-5: doi:10.1045/may2006-letters.

Bailey, A., Back, G. (2006) 'LibX: a Firefox extension for enhanced library access', *Library High Tech,* 24-2: 290.

Bell, S. (2006) 'More on XC From David Lindahl', *ARCLog,* posted 17 May: available at *http://acrllog .org/2006/05/17/more-on-xc-from-david-lindahl/.*

Book Burro (2006) Available at *http://www.bookburro.org.*

Bowen, J., *et al.* (2004) 'Serial failure', *Charleston Advisor,* 5-3: 48–50.

Bowen, J. and Lindahl, D. (2005) 'Metadata that supports real user needs'. Available at *http://www.lita.org/ ala/lita/litaevents/litanationalforum2005sanjoseca/57_ Lindahl_Bowen.ppt.*

Breeding, M. (2007) 'An update on open source ILS', *Computers in Libraries,* 27-3: 27–9.

Burke, G., Germain, C.A. and Van Ullen, M.K. (2003)

'URLs in the OPAC: integrating or disintegrating research libraries' catalogs', *Journal of Academic Librarianship*, 29-5: 290–7.

Calhoun, K. (2006) *The Changing Nature of the Catalog and its Integration with Other Discovery Tools*. Ithaca, New York, USA: Cornell University Press.

Carter, J. (2007) Personal communication, 24 January.

Cohen, L. (2004) 'Issues in URL management', *Information Technology and Libraries*, June: 42–9.

Culling, J. (2007) *Link Resolvers and the Serials Supply Chain: Final Project Report for the UKSG*. Oxfrd, UK: Scholarly Information Strategies.

Dempsey, L. (2006) 'The library catalogue in the new discovery environment: some thoughts', *Ariadne*, 48: available at *http://www/ariadne.ac.uk/issue48/dempsey/*.

Elsevier Corporation (2002) *Elsevier Editors Update*, Issue 2. Available at *http://www.elsevier.com/wps/find/editorsinfo.editors/editors_update/issue2c* (accessed 22 April 2005).

Herrera, G. (2007) 'Metasearching and beyond: implementation experiences and advice from an academic library', *Information Technology and Libraries*, available at *http://www.ala.org/ala/lita/litapublications/ital/262007/2602jun/herrera.pdf*.

IBM (2007) *New to SOA and Web services*. Available at *http://www.ibm.com/developerworks/webservices/newto/websvc.html*.

JISC (2007) *Information Environment*. Available at *http://www.jisc.ac.uk/whatwedo/themes/information_environment.aspx*.

JISC (2007) *JISC Integrated Information Environment Committee*. Available at *http://www.jisc.ac.uk/aboutus/committees/sub_committees/jiie.aspx*.

JISC (undated) *JISC Linking digital libraries with VLEs programme*. Available at *http://www.jisc.ac.uk/whatwedo/programmes/programme_divle.aspx*.

Johnson, R.K. (2007) 'In Google's broad wake: taking responsibility for shaping the global digital library', *ARL: A Bimonthly Report*, 250.

Kohl, D.F. and Sanville, T. (2006) 'More bang for the buck: increasing the effectiveness of library expenditures', *Library Trends*, 54: 394–410.

Koppel, T. (2006) *An Introduction to the Rapidly Changing World of ERM Standards*. Verde/Ex Libris. Available at *http://www.exlibrisgroup.com/files/Publications/Rapidly changingworldofERMstandards.pdf*.

Landesmann, B. and Weston, B. (1999) "Barbarism is the absence of standards': applying standards to untangle the electronic jungle', *Serials Librarian*, 36 (3/4): 515–23.

Lindahl, D. and Suszczynski, J. (2005) *Rethinking Metasearch for a Better User Experience*. NISO OpenUrl workshop. Available at *http://docushare.lib.rochester.edu/docushare/dsweb/Services/Document-20513*.

Livingston, J., Sanford, D. and Bretthauer, D. (2006) 'A comparison of OpenURL link resolvers: the results of a University of Connecticut Libraries environmental scan', *Library Collections, Acquisitions, & Technical Services*, 30: 179–201.

LOCKSS (2007) *Lots of Copies Keeps Stuff Safe*. Available at *http://www.lockss.org/lockss/Home*.

McCracken, P. (2003) 'A comparison of print and electronic journal holdings in academic and public libraries', *Libri*, 53: 237–41.

Miller, L., Klemperer, K. and Hawkins, L. (2006) 'What is ONIX for serials? What poetential does it have for the serials workflow?', *Serials Reivew*, 32-1: 40.

Misek, M. (2004) 'Highwire Press: keeping the scholars in

scholarly publishing', *Econtentmag*, July/August: available at *http://www.econtentmag.com/Articles/ArticlePrint.aspx?ArticleID=6872.*

Nardini, B. (2007) *The Book Vendor Perspective.* US Library of Congress Working Group on the Future of Bibliographic Control/Coutts Information Services. Available at *http://www.couttsinfo.com/enews/current/news_vendorperspective.htm.*

National and State Libraries Australasia (2007) *The Big Bang: Creating the new library universe.* Available at *http://www.nsla.org.au/publications/papers/2007/pdf/NSLA.Discussion-Paper-20070629-The.Big.Bang..creating.the.new.library.universe.pdf.*

NISO (2007) *In Development.* Available at *http://www.niso.org/committees/index.html.*

NISO (2007) *VIEWS Initiative: VIEWS: Vendor Initiative for Enabling Web Services.* Available at *http://www.nisco.org/committees/VIEWS/VIEWS-info.html.*

NISO Web Services and Practices Working Group (2006a) *Best Practices for Designing Web Services in the Library Context.* Bethesda, Maryland, USA: NISO Press.

NISO Web Services and Practices Working Group (2006b) *Meeting minutes, 26 June 2006 conference call.* Available at *http://www.niso.org/communittees/Services/Services-minutes.html.*

OCLC (2007) *OCLC to pilot WorldCat Local.* Available at *http://www.oclc.org/news/releases/200659.htm.*

OCLC Abstracts (2005) *OCLC Members Council takes a closer look at the global library landscape.* Available at *http://www5.oclc.org/downloads/design/abstracts/05312005/memberscouncil.htm.*

OCLC WorldCat (undated) *xISBN (web service).* Available at *http://www.worldcat.org/affiliate/webservices/xisbn/app.jsp.*

Ort, E., Brydon, S. and Basler, M. (2007) *Mashup Styles,*

Part 1: Server-Side Mashups. Sun Developer Network. Available at *http://java.sun.com/developer/technicalArticles/J2EE/mashup_1/.*

Pace, A.K. (2004) *Dis-Integrated Library Systems: Promise and Peril.* Available at *http://library.acadiau.ca/access2004/presentations/pace.ppt.*

Pace, A.K. (2007) 'What's the Big Deal?', *American Libraries*, 38-3: 30–2.

PCMag.com Encyclopedia (undated) *Mashup.* Available at *http://www.pcmag.com/encyclopedia_term/0,2542,t=mashup&i=55949,00.asp.*

Pinfield, S., *et al.* (1998) 'Realizing the hybrid library', *D-Lib Magazine*, October: available at *http:www.dlib.org/dlib/october98/10pinfield.html.*

Pollard, M. (2005) *Federated Searching at Cal. State.* ALA National Conference resource. Available at *http://www.ala.org/ala/lita/litamembership/litaigs/internetresource/FedSearchingCalState.ppt.*

Rhyno, A. (1999) *The end of the ILS – or where does OLAF come from? InsideOlita*, posted 16 October 2003: available at *http://webvoy.uwindsor.ca:8087/artblog/librarycog/1066337683.*

Scholar Portal (2005) *Scholars Portal.* Available at *http://www.scholarsportal.info.*

Serials Solutions (undated) *Understanding E-Resource Access and Management Services.* Available at *http://www.serialssolutions.com/downloads/ss_erams_brochure_P3026N-0307.pdf.*

Shank, J.D. (2003) 'The emergence of learning objects: the reference librarian's role', *Research Strategies*, 19: 193–203.

Shibboleth Project (2007) *Shibboleth.* Available at *http://shibboleth.internet2.edu/.*

Singer, R. (2006) 'About Ross Singer's Umlaut', *OCLC*, available at *http://www.oclc.org/research/announcements/features/ umlaut-about.htm* (accessed 26 March 2007).

Singer, R. (2007) *Re: link resolvers as loosely coupled systems for holdings?* Available at *http:// serials.infomotions.com/ngc4lib/archive/2007/200709/18 18.html.*

Stanley, T. (2006) 'Web 2.0: supporting library user. QA Focus', *Library Technology Reports*, May/June.

Stranack, K. (2006) 'CUFTS: An open source alternative for serials management', *Serials Librarian*, 51-2: 29.

Stanford Encyclopedia of Philosophy (2007) *About the Stanford Encyclopedia of Philosophy*. Available at *http://plato.stanford.edu/about.html.*

Storey, T (2006) 'Moving to the network level', *NEXT Space*, 4: 7–11.

Tennant, R. (2005) 'Lipstick on a pig', *Library Journal*, 130-7: 34.

Tennant, R. (2007) *Trouble in Online Paradise: Analysis of MARC 856 Usage at One Institution*. Available at *http://roytennant.com/proto/856/analysis.html.*

Thorhauge, J. (2003) 'The personal library: integrating the library in the networking society', in *Emerging Visions for Access in the Twenty-first Century Library*. Council on Library and Information Resources: available at *http://www.clir.org/pubs/reports/pub119/thorhauge.html.*

Tillett, B. (2004) *What is FRBR: A conceptual Model for the Bibliographic Universe*. Washington, D.C., USA: Library of Congress Cataloging Distribution Service.

Udell, J. (2002) *The LibraryLookup Project*. Available at *http://weblog.infoworld.com/udell/stories/2002/12/11/lib rarylookup.html.*

Udell, J. (2005) 'Service-oriented architectures', *InfoWorld*,

27-11: 48.

Van de Sompel, H., Young, J. and Hickey, T. (2003) 'Using the OAI-PMH...differently', *D-Lib Magazine*, 9-7/8: available at *http://www.dlib.org/dlib/july03/young/07young.html*.

VTLS (2004) *"VIEWS" A newly created Vendor Initiative for Enabling Web Services announced*. Available at *http://www.vtls.com/Corporate/Releases/2004/21.shtml*.

Vondracek, R. (2007) 'Comfort and convenience? Why students choose alternatives to the library', *Libraries and the Academy*, 7.3: 277–93.

Wakimoto, J.C., Walker, D.S. and Dabbour, K.S. (2006) 'The myths and realities of SFX in academic libraries', *The Journal of Academic Librarianship*, 32-2: 127–36.

Wang, J. and Schroeder, A.T. Jr. (2005) 'The subscription agent as e-journal intermediary', *Serials Review*, 31-1: 20–7.

Webster, P. (2002) 'Remote patron validation: posting a proxy server at the DIGITAL doorway', *Computers in Libraries*, 22-8: 18–24.

Webster, P. (2004) 'Metasearching in an academic environment', *Online*, 28-2: 20–3.

Webster, P. (2007a) 'Challenges for federated searching', *Internet Reference Services Quarterly*, 12(3/4): 357–68.

Webster, P. (2007b) 'The library in your toolbar', *Library Journal*, 132-12: 30–2.

Wilson, A. (Ed.) (2003) *The 2003 OCLC Environmental Scan: Pattern Recognition*. Dublin Ohio, USA: OCLC Online Computer Library Centre, Inc.

Winblad, A.L., Edwards, S.D. and King, D.R. (1990) *Object-Oriented Software*. Reading Massachusetts, USA: Addison-Wesley.

Zagar, C. (2007) 'Unlocking library subscriptions', *Library Journal Net Connect*, 132.

Index

Printed in the United States
123186LV00002B/105-110/P

9 781843 343684